LEAVING ROLLINGSTONE

LEAVING

LEAVING ROLLINGSTONE

ROLLINGSTONE

a memoir

KEVIN FENTON

www.mhspress.org

The Minnesota Historical Society Press is a member of the Association of American University Presses.

Manufactured in the United States of America

10 9 8 7 6 5 4 3 2 1

∞ The paper used in this publication meets the minimum requirements of the American National Standard for Information Sciences—Permanence for Printed Library Materials, ANSI Z39.48-1984.

International Standard Book Number
ISBN: 978-1-68134-065-4 (pbk)
ISBN: 978-0-87351-913-7 (cloth)
ISBN: 978-0-87351-915-1 (e-book)

Library of Congress Cataloging-in-Publication Data
Fenton, Kevin, 1959-
Leaving Rollingstone : a memoir / Kevin Fenton.
pages cm
Summary: "Leaving Rollingstone is the story of how a Twin Cities advertising writer and novelist reclaimed the enduring values and surprising vitality of his small-town Minnesota boyhood"—Provided by publisher.
ISBN 978-0-87351-913-7 (cloth : alk. paper)—ISBN 978-0-87351-915-1 (ebook)
1. Fenton, Kevin, 1959—Childhood and youth 2. Copy writers—Minnesota—Biography. 3. Authors, American—21st century—Biography. 4. Rollingstone (Minn.) I. Title.
PS3606.E5843Z46 2013
813'.6—dc23
[B] 2013016939

This and other Minnesota Historical Society Press books are available from popular e-book vendors.

To John Kendrick, who was a friend since I knew what a friend was

To the memory of Bill Schuth, who lived the values I try to describe here

And, always, to Ellen

LEAVING ROLLINGSTONE

I ROLLINGSTONE

THE GOLDEN AGE

I TEND TO REDUCE MY CHILDHOOD TO A BEATLES MOVIE—an edited, accelerated, saturated, and scripted happiness.

Before dawn, late November, almost winter, a kitchen in a farmhouse on a ridge above Rollingstone, Minnesota, a village in the southeastern part of the state, in country that looks more like New England than anything in the Midwest.

I am still sleepy, so more of the world seeps in. The windows in the kitchen look out toward the machine shed, yet I can't see anything but the reflection of the halo-shaped kitchen light, the blue flame of our gas stove, the tutti-frutti-speckled linoleum, and my family, standing in bathrobes. We all stand on the floor vents, aligning ourselves along the wall like the saints in church. If I were to place my hand on the glass, I would feel its chill. But I'm standing away from it, the metal floor vents embossing my bare feet, the air from the vent heating my shins and tickling my pajama bottoms. My mom walks from person to person and refills our cocoa. Then she makes another trip and gives us toast. It looks as if she is serving us communion. When I dip the toast, the margarine floats and glows on top of the cocoa. I eat the triangle of cocoa-soaked toast in one bite.

We leave our mugs in the sink, sprint upstairs, and tug on jeans and flannels. We step into boots in the entryway; we run out the door; the chill air surprises our lungs and smoothes our skin. We hurry, almost running, goofing around in the way that we have learned from Beatles movies, yelling, mock-threatening. The yard light illuminates the graveled driveway and grassy strip in front of the barn. We pass the shed, then the chicken coop. My brother Dennis turns right, into the barn. Dad follows behind us. He limps. Hip replacements have shortened one leg, but the latest operation appears to be taking. He is careful. At this time of year in southern Minnesota, the ground can ice over.

Dad is careful; we're not. Dawn tints the sky and reveals the horizon. We jog into the barnyard, stepping in shit, following the strangely thin cow trails, darting into the nibbled land, past the leafless birch trees, wiry raspberry brambles, and dry milkweeds. We sprint. We locate the cows and urge them toward the barn. Now, we slow because the cows, not having seen Beatles films, take their time. There are fewer than thirty of them, so we know their grandmotherly names: Abigail, Bessie. Because they have names, we love them a little too much. When the cows are in their stalls, the girls and I walk up to the house. Dennis and Dad stay behind to milk them. We stop at the chicken coop—a cave of straw and poop, lit by bare bulbs, toothy with beaks and claws. We collect the eggs.

The girls put on records while we get ready for school. The candy-colored, fragile 45s spin like a county fair ride; the needle skates and scratches above them. Herman's Hermits' "No Milk Today." Uncool but surprisingly beautiful. The Ohio Express's "Yummy Yummy Yummy." Uncool but surprisingly fun. Dennis runs in after finishing the milking and quickly gets ready. He washes and then changes from his farmer clothes into penny loafers, blue jeans, and an untucked oxford shirt. He Brylcreems his hair and sticks the comb in his pocket. He looks like one of the Beach Boys.

My oldest sister, Maureen, and my mom have left for Winona, where Mom works in the hospital and Maureen attends college. Everyone else is ready. I follow them out to the pickup. Because there is only a front seat, we either cram together or I hop into the open back. Memory sputters here, so I imagine what happens next. Dennis says something like, "We *really wanted* you to sit in the front seat with us . . . but . . ." And here Dennis parodies a customs agent who has noticed a difficulty he wishes he could dismiss but knows he must address. He winces; he visibly cogitates.

He finally speaks again. "It seems that, well . . . it just seems that you . . . might not be . . . *cool* enough."

Colleen says, "Oh, Dennis, stop being so mean." But even she knows that his threat is about as mean as the crust on an apple pie.

"Okay, this time, you're in. But try to get *a lot cooler* by tomorrow morning." We cram into the front seat and head into town. As we descend the hill and approach the zag we call Devil's Curve, Dennis accelerates, to scare the girls. They scream as they look out over the tree-interrupted drop that separates them from the Speltzes' pasture. There is no glass in the window in the back of the pickup. Cold air swirls behind our heads; heated air blasts toward us. We could stick some cardboard in there, but that wouldn't be cool, either.

After school, Colleen and Sheila dance in the living room to Freddy Cannon, who sings the theme to the teenybopper show *Where the Action Is.* The girls Frug and Twist and Pony to a voice—tinny, manic—that sounds like a transistor radio. He wants to take them where the action is, on the Sunset Strip. Later in the show, young men in Revolutionary War costumes—wigs, tricornered hats—play guitars and keyboards on the beach.

At night, Dennis and the girls ricochet knock-knock jokes from their beds, between our room and theirs.

"Knock knock."
"Who's there?"
"Pecan."
"Pecan who?"
"Pecan someone your own size."

"Knock knock."
"Who's there?"
"Gorilla."
"Gorilla who?"
"Gorilla me a cheese sandwich."

The point of the jokes is the awfulness of the jokes. We are all already tucked in. The lights are out. Our voices frolic like cartoon ghosts.

I watch this private movie of my childhood when my adult mind becomes ugly with the present—when my resentments bore even me. My mind tends toward the obsessive. I don't solve problems so much as erode them. But when I remember the farm, my thoughts simplify until they are not uniquely human. I feel mute and sensitive to love. I feel as if I am nosing among happy presence. I feel with the wistfulness of a beloved dog: *I liked these humans. I am sad that they have left.*

This remembered, composited day was not as simple as I remember. I was seven. I missed things.

Farming is simple only to those who've never tried it. A farm is a factory open to the weather, with a delicate inventory and a fickle market. It requires seven-days-a-week work, favorable weather, heavy lifting, substantial credit lines, and tricky decisions on equipment upgrades. Spend too little on these upgrades and you fall behind. Spend too much and the debt can cripple you.

The seemingly simple world of hay bales and manure was whipsawed by invisibilities: the slippery paradoxes of agricultural economics, the esoteric protections of agricultural law, which encoded Jefferson's love of the family farm into a thousand exceptions. Understand these oddities and you could hedge against the vagaries of weather and economics; your hard work could become that legally blessed thing called a corporation; you could pass your farm on without bankrupting your children. Fail to understand them and they become one more storm that gathers on the horizon. Nearly twenty years later, I would study agricultural law and get one of a handful of law school As, but I never went into law. It was too late; my truest clients no longer needed me.

After we had all left for school and my father was alone in the farmhouse, his past may have strobed in his mind: It was 1938 in Cabery, Illinois. His basketball team had won a district tournament. He and his teammates packed into one of those bulbous 1930s cars. I suspect the boys were that rare thing: young people aware of their youth, carbonated with victory, giddy with the fluidity of their layups, the precision of their set shots, the deftness of their passes. As they drove along, celebrating and taunting each other, the driver dropped a lit cigarette by his foot. It jiggled and glowed by the accelerator. He bent to pick it up, revealing sky to those in the backseat. The land was flat. The sky in front of them was huge, so huge it felt like grief; its immensity evaporated the human. In that moment, the car swerved, struck a stone historical marker, and detonated.

As Dad awoke on the pavement, tangled in wreckage, his lungs surprised by the winter air, his eyes confronted by a strange perspective, his body jolted with shock, his muscles raw to the air, he must have thought, in something that wasn't quite a sentence and that memory immediately blanched: *everything has changed.* He saw blood on the highway. He could not move one leg.

And everything *had* changed. My father's lips and nose had detached from his face and had to be sewn back on. He also had broken his hip. One of the boys had launched through the roof and died. Another died soon thereafter.

Dad would spend the next five years in hospitals.

In 1966, at our kitchen table, even in this day in what I think of as a golden age, he swallows a Darvon, a narcotic related to methadone, for the pain.

As my mother lay in bed that morning in 1966, the future may have strobed in her mind, and it did not reassure her. Hours before, exhausted but still wakeful with caffeine, she had forced her eyes shut and finally sunk into sleep. All through the night, the clock ticked; the hands traversed the circle. A bell tizzied in her ear. Consciousness intruded on her silty sleep, like a hook jerking through water. She started to move to quiet the bell, but she couldn't, not quite yet, not right now. Then she decided, quickly, that she must. She grasped the alarm and shut it off. She let her head fall back. For those few minutes, her head settling into the pillow, her mind puddling and vulnerable, she allowed herself to feel how afraid she really was. Maurice's latest hip operation had been no more successful than the earlier ones. Medical bills mounted. Too much was being asked of Dennis.

But fear was a movie she didn't have time to watch. She had to keep her part of a bargain she had made more than twenty years before. She stood across from my father in Holy Trinity Church in Rollingstone on a weekday, surrounded by their big families, the church brightened by children who had been let out of school to attend the wedding, and she recited marriage vows freighted with an intimacy few brides have with their betrothed: she had been my dad's nurse. She had read his charts. His hip had been broken and repaired, but because of the damage to his circulation, it was starved for blood, so it would be slow to repair itself. She had seen his disfigured body, the purple continent of damage around his hip and shin. She was a woman who took words seriously, who would stand before a Hallmark display and read card after card until she found the rhymes she felt in her heart. When she said, "For better or for worse," she agreed to something specific. She said to me years later, when I tried to discover more about our time on the farm, that "I knew when I married your dad that I might have to support him."

In 1966, at 5:30 in the morning, my father stirred next to her. She said something like, "Another day. I'll make breakfast."

My golden age in 1966 was for my parents a few months of relative luck. Between 1960 and 1970, Dad would have his hip replaced twelve times. Mom would pack his bags forty-seven times, for forty-seven hospitalizations. She counted.

I never practiced law. Instead, I went into advertising. I don't believe that advertising is a lie, although it's sometimes a fantasy. At its best, though, a good ad is the happiest and simplest of truths.

For decades, since long before I wrote my first ad, I have been compiling this movie trailer that I call my memories. You would think a movie trailer would be simple and satisfying, and in some ways it is. I was raised by good people in a good place. But I see some surprising things when I look hard from the perspective of my various adult selves. As an ad man, I realize that what I've always thought of as a rustic memory of a family farm brims with the shine and pulse of popular culture. As someone who teaches fiction, I always thought I knew the hero of this story—my dad, struggling to keep the farm. But my thoughts on the subject have grown more complicated. As someone who has left the village for the city, I find myself wondering what I have taken with me—and what I lost forever when I left Rollingstone.

* * *

When I try to sum up my Rollingstone experience in the glib way you sum up whole portions of your life during conversation with near-strangers at Christmas open houses and client dinners, I say, "Until I was twelve, I thought *goddamnLuxembourger* was one word." It usually gets a laugh. It usually gets a laugh from the Luxembourgers themselves.

Rollingstone was 95 percent Luxembourger. During the First World War, the young men from Rollingstone could still speak Luxembourgish to relatives they met in Europe. Eventually, a few non-Luxembourg families, including my mother's (who were largely Irish), moved in to enroll their children in the free parish school. My father agreed to move there because he wanted to farm, and that was possible there. He became known as the Irishman. But in the sixties, a dozen names still proliferated in the pamphlet-sized phone book. Off the top of my head, I recall five Speltz families who owned four farms.

I think the reason *goddamnLuxembourger* prompted laughs is that it represents such a strangely intramural prejudice. The Herbers and the Hengels and the Speltzes and the Kreidemachers and the Kronebusches shared my family's culture: we all attended the same school, said the same prayers, did the same work, favored the same brand of tractors, shopped in the same stores, watched the same television programs, and anticipated the same heaven. They all, basically, seemed to like us, and we liked them.

To get a sense of how deep Rollingstone's Luxembourger roots go, read *Rollingstone: A Luxembourgish Village in Minnesota,* written by Rollingstone native and City University of New York professor Mary Nilles and published in 1983. The book lovingly describes the project of Rollingstone: how the town was founded in the 1860s, in the valley that the evicted Dakota named *E-yan-o-min-man-wat-pah,* "a stone that had been rolling"; how, although the founders lacked the isolating zeal of religious sects, the village attempted to continue the Old World rather than to create a new one. America is too glibly viewed as a place to start over. The early settlers left Luxembourg not because they wanted to reject it, but because they could not find jobs or land. A nostalgia slowed and sweetened the town from the very beginning. The first settlers missed Luxembourg; they were homesick, which is to say they were heartbroken. Rollingstone was born as an extension of Europe.

In Nilles's book, time stops at about 1920, and this reflects the wish of Rollingstone's founders that things stay the same. Our family wasn't Luxembourger, but we wanted the town to stay as it was, too.

What amazes me most about *Rollingstone* are the photographs. The cover photo emphasizes the link to old Europe: women sit demurely in billowing skirts and blossoming hats; and men in vests, bow ties, boaters, or bowlers are arranged along the branches of a tree just behind the women. Only the plants—scruffy pasture grass, complex ferns, swarming leaves—are familiar. It's less an American scene than the subject matter of the Impressionists. But the names are familiar. Most of the men are named Rivers. The women's names include one Rivers, and also a Speltz, a Kramer, and a Dietrich—all names I knew from grade school. I was looking at the great-grandparents of Butter Rivers, whose dad ran the creamery.

The faces in the book are even more startling than the names. The people I knew in 1960s Rollingstone weren't born yet, but their faces were: the shadowed eyes of certain of the Herbers; the fine features of some Hengels; the intelligent squint of Mr. Rivers; the doughy face and curly hair of Mary Nilles's brother, Myron; the sharp, serious faces and dark hair of the Kronebusches. And it was these repeating names and recurring faces that could—when things otherwise weren't going his way—bother my dad and cause him to mumble, in the vague direction of his problems, *goddamnLuxembourgers.*

* * *

While Rollingstone was 95 percent Luxembourger, it was 100 percent Catholic. I breathed this Catholicism when the smoke from censers swung at certain Masses sweetened the air. I felt this Catholicism in the bumpy flow of rosary beads in my hands and in the strain in my knees, which trembled from kneeling too long. I sensed it in the rhyming morbid prayers I mumbled before bed ("Now I lay me down to sleep./I pray the Lord my soul to keep/If I should die before I wake,/I pray the Lord my soul to take"). I saw it in the curtseying flames of votive candles, in the mannequin intensity of the saints in the church, in the Virgin with her heart on the outside of her body, in the jeweled stories told by stained-glass windows. I heard it in the tolling of church bells and the tinkling of the sanctus bells the altar boys rang at intervals. In our house, frosted glass hands prayed on dressers, statues of the Virgin calmed the buffet, Christs writhed on crucifixes on the wall, Communion candles waited in the purgatory of attics, and rosaries were as ubiquitous as house keys.

Catholicism even shaped our play. When Colleen and Sheila were old enough to read but not to reason, they placed apples on the cross as an offering for Jesus. They found a note that said that Jesus preferred Hershey bars. Thinking they were witness to a miracle, they told my mom. Mom recognized Dennis's handwriting. She had to tell them about how she did the same thing with raisins when she was a little girl, and how her older brothers had pulled the same trick on her.

But the Catholicism I was born into wasn't all playful. A document that I discovered in the basement of the Winona County Historical Society embodied the harsher side of this Catholicism. Its letters' indentations suggested the *whack, whack* of manual typing. The document—unsigned, undated, apparently created in 1954—sketches the history of Holy Trinity Church—the first settlers, the first Mass, the first church building, the first resident priest, and then, twenty-five years later, the school. The school, so solid and central in my boyhood world, is surprisingly tenuous, "an ambitious project in so small a parish."

By 1954, the "ambitious project" had graduated only 256 students, yet the report notes that "Rollingstone has given to the Church eight priests, twenty sisters, one brother, one seminarian now in second philosophy." One out of every eight students who graduated from Holy Trinity became a priest, nun, or brother.

The report ends with an exhortation: "But that noble history is also a challenge to this generation. God alone knows how much faith and courage may be required in the lives of those who now face the uncertain future."

An even more interesting document can be found within the parishioners' report. To fortify its call to faith, the history quotes the July–August issue of the *Social Justice Review:*

> These are extraordinary times, and call for extraordinary Catholics. Otherwise, in countries such as ours, extinction is a possibility. The old faith is at war with the new paganism.

The prose reminds me of nothing so much as the times when my mother would grab our wrists when we tried to steal the raw potatoes she was preparing. She wasn't a big woman, but her grasp was amazingly strong, and we could never get away. Similarly, the prose here is all knuckle and tendon and assertion.

I don't want to seize on a few hypocrisies—say, the German cardinals saluting the Führer at Nuremburg—because, when pushed, I'd have to admit that my own beliefs aren't free from the toxins of contradiction and denial. And I do not want to fall into the time chauvinism that reflexively views the present as enlightened and the past as so much superstition. If "pagan" is viewed as simply non- or nominally Christian, the world probably is pagan.

What frightens me here—and in the larger article—is the sense of a man ossifying into a God. War gives us permission to kill, a power that is normally reserved to the Deity. Lutherans were condemned to hell. A son or daughter who married a Lutheran was disowned. Protestants with children who thought about moving to Rollingstone were pulled aside and discouraged by a committee of townsmen because we could not provide them with a public school.

Catholicism was our calendar and our clock. We observed holy days of obligation such as All Souls' Day, the day after Halloween when we prayed for the souls of the dead, and the Feast of the Assumption, which celebrated Mary's bodily ascension into heaven. We waited for Christ during Advent and deprived ourselves during Lent by giving up candy or TV. The Masses of Holy Week—Holy Thursday, with the washing of the priest's feet; stark Good Friday, without music or Communion; the vigil of Holy Saturday; the joyous release of Easter—felt like travel. We lived in Rollingstone and Biblical Palestine.

I can't remember the name of a single mayor. I can remember the name of every priest. I was raised in a theocracy.

* * *

I was born into stories—stories told at our kitchen table as teenagers fought over pizza and poured themselves fizzing pop, as adults played joshingly competitive games of 500 Rummy over coffee and caramel rolls. Our stories picked up the rhythm of the cartoon, the energy of the pop song, the quick cut of the sitcom, and the giddiness of karaoke. Maureen would sing "The Lion Sleeps Tonight." Dad would sing whatever novelty song was popular at the time. While some people are nostalgic for a more leisurely time, I'm nostalgic for a more accelerated one.

Even the explanation of my name arrived as an anecdote. *Before you were born, Dad took all of the kids to Dairy Queen and promised them that if they voted for the name Kevin, they could get anything they wanted. Mom wanted you to be named Maurice after Dad, but he thought that being a junior put too much pressure on a kid. Mom never had a chance.*

And I learned about the rest of the family through such snippets: *Mom once looked out the window and saw Dennis chasing Maureen with a rake, like Wile E. Coyote chasing the Road Runner.*

(Moral: Dennis is almost comically competitive.) When the girls wanted to play with Maureen, she told them they were going to play "family" and that family consisted of the following Warholian performance art: get in the car and wait the fifteen minutes it would take to get to a theater in Winona, come back into the house and "watch a movie" on the television for two hours, "get sick" and take sadistically unsweetened Watkins medicine, and then go to bed indefinitely while Maureen goes about her business. (Moral: Maureen is aloof and darkly comic.) Sheila and Colleen once, at Sheila's insistence, painted themselves with mud and presented themselves to Mom. (The girls are a yin-yang duo, with Sheila being the troublemaker.)

My parents' backstory was exuberantly sketched in:

Your mom studied nursing in Winona and then Rochester because, while she wanted to attend the University of Minnesota and study journalism, her father thought there were too many Communists there and forbade it.

Your dad announced to your mom on their second date that he was going to marry her.

When your mother was pregnant with Dennis, diabetes swelled her waist to sixty inches, and Dad joked that he could just "roll her down the hill." When your mom was on bed rest with you, bed rest meant that she didn't iron the starched shirts your dad wore in the field.

Mom and Dad used to go dancing at the Altura Fire Hall on Saturday nights in the fifties. Mom was a timid, tentative dancer because, when she was a little girl, the priest told her that dancing at non-Catholic events was a mortal sin. So the whole evening, Dad would hold her by the waist and carry her around the floor, reassuring her, "It's okay, Holly. I've got you."

The moral of these anecdotes? We suffer but shine.

These stories mixed with darker ones. Dad's problems with his hip and his health, in remission for much of the fifties, resurfaced. Surgeries failed. He might not have been able to continue farming. So your mother pushed herself even harder than a farm wife and working mother of the fifties normally would. For a time, with four children under ten at home, she worked graveyard shifts (eleven at night until seven in the morning) until, unable to sleep during the day, her mind fraying from exhaustion, Dad insisted she take a more humane shift. Her diabetes jeopardized her pregnancies, and in the years she bore five living children, she also miscarried three times. Once Dad had to carry her while she hemorrhaged between her legs, into the hospital, past the protesting admissions desk, to Winona's overmatched facilities. In the ambulance speeding toward Rochester, Mom's blood pressure sank, her self drifted away from her body, and she negotiated with God, asking him to save her because she had four children to take care of.

I was her fifth child, delivered a month early, via C-section.

This occasioned more stories: *Your birth was announced on the intercom at Holy Trinity School. When you were a baby, we would carry you around on a blanket and sing "Hail, Hail to the King."*

* * *

In a sense, I was also born into cinematography. My image of the years before my birth takes its tints from the silver of movies, the grey of TV shows, the halftones of newspapers, and the monochrome of family photographs. I know better now but I still visualize the world before my birth as black and white. Then, when I was born, by the evidence of the family photographs and the culture at large, color flooded the world.

No wonder they announced my birth over the intercom. I have a powerful sense of being born lucky. I wish I could say the same for my parents.

TRASH CANS WERE MY FIRST anthologies. I toddled amid backyard ones that stood like burnt altars, crusted with carbon and pocked with holes. The trash cans held exploded egg shells, the doughy cardboard of egg packaging, greased butter wrappers, and bloody butcher paper. They held language that I could not yet decode: manic cereal boxes, stylized cake mixes, and the balloony colors of bread wrappers. Once the trash can got too full, we would ignite the contents. The grease in the bacon and butter packaging would hiss; the bread wrappers would shiver and melt; the paper would flare; the heat would shimmer; the smoke would waft; and then the fire would subside, and our trash would become ashes.

Flame was much more with us than it is now: businesses gave out matchbooks decorated with their logos. The world was more fragrant then: my parents' friends smoked cigarettes in stores and living rooms; Dad indulged in Dutch Masters cigars; in autumn, people burned leaves.

EXILES ON CREAMERY STREET

1962. THE VILLAGE OF ROLLINGSTONE HAD JUST HAD a picnic when a cloudburst pummeled us, soaked our clothing, and saturated the green of the grass. Everyone else ran for the pavilion or their cars. But because the wind had gusted and blown the yellow plasticware from the tables, my siblings and I suddenly had a job to do. We swarmed after the escaping utensils as they collected under the merry-go-round, flew under the swings, sprayed up against the tennis court. Maybe because I was three, this invasion felt giddy, like being tickled by the sky; the utensils became exclamation marks. Five kids pursued five hundred things. Plucking forks and knives from the ground, we glimpsed the shiny leaves of broadleaf plantain and a frizzy, yellow-flowered grass. But we had to keep running and lunging and grabbing and screaming. The hysterical sky let us act hysterically.

The memory is innocent, but something shivers beneath it. It isn't the giddy freedom that has caused me to remember it; it is the color scheme. The green of the grass and the yellow of the forks scattered in the park suggest the green and yellow of tractors, the green and yellow of corn, and, thus, the farm we abandoned. We moved into Rollingstone because one of Dad's surgeries had gone particularly badly. We sold the farm to an in-law who rented it to our old neighbors, the Herbers, while they built a new house on their farm. Our family talked about the farm all the time. If families had mission statements back then, "regain the farm" would have been ours. Dennis, who had followed Dad everywhere, spent his summer working on the farm of another family on the ridge above Rollingstone.

Here, in Rollingstone, we hosted the picnic because the town had given Dad part-time work taking care of the park. Dennis and the girls helped Dad. He couldn't sprint after forks; he couldn't howl and dart and dive.

My memories of town are of motion as cheerful and alarming as an amusement park. Children scurried around me, playing "Annie, Annie, Over." Colleen and Sheila and their friends propelled bikes, sprinted to tag each other, lofted kickballs, and squealed and refused to be called home for dinner. Mrs. Rinn across the street yelled, "Fran-cis! Fra-a-a-n-cis!," but Franny Rinn, who was five, didn't come home when he was supposed to. Why should he? I've never seen so much fun in one city block.

From where we lived, on this street as comfortable as a driveway, I could waddle the hundred feet to the creamery and "charge" ice cream. I could venture a block and try to buy candy from Mr. Arnoldy. I could mount a little expedition out our backyard, across the street and schoolyard, past the convent, and into the church during Mass—Colleen was supposed to be watching me but wasn't—in a tie and diaper combo I'd improvised for the occasion. Father Majures would halt his Latin. The parishioners would suppress laughter as my parents, startled in their pew, whisked me home.

Our family mourned the farm, and as a three-year-old, I absorbed their mourning. The family myth—also told over pop and popcorn—was that Sheila loved it here in Rollingstone. It suited whatever was in her that thrived in the noisiness of towns, in their near lives and bright commerce. But while I shared the loss I could feel in my dad and my brother, I also loved this town.

Sometimes we would ride out of town in our Ford Falcon that smelled like plastic and dust and sunlight to the border of my three-year-old world, toward the Kendricks' and Literskis', toward the horizon where my mother worked and where we shopped, and I would see the town dump, a mound filled with mattresses softened with use, with radios that had once channeled Roosevelt, with wringer washers and irreparable cars and senile farm equipment and worn-out clothes and libraries of forties and fifties magazines and busted toys.

As part of his deal with the town—which I now realize was a jobs program of one, an act of tactful charity on the part of the goddamnLuxembourgers—Dad worked at the dump a couple of hours a day. Refuse needed to be sorted into salable metals and parts, piles untangled, the oldest remnants buried. Dad wasn't given to metaphor, which was a good thing, but the place and what it represented couldn't help but seep into his thoughts. Dumps aren't subtle. By the time we'd moved into the village, Dad had gone through several replacement hips, which meant that parts of his body had been thrown away.

But Dad was jaunty about the operations. He gave one of the spikes that had been taken out of his hip to a hospital roommate, a kid who'd been injured in a motorcycle accident. The kid used the spike as the shift on his cycle. It's quite possible that even today, somewhere, someone looks at a vintage Harley, notices the stick shift, and says, "What the hell?"

There must have been times when the powerlessness brought on by his infirmities overwhelmed him. One day when it was just Dad and me at home, I hid his cane while he napped. He yelled at me from the bed but couldn't leave it. He was trapped until Mom got home, an exile from his own house.

* * *

In the fall of 1963, after the harvest, we moved back to the farm. But before we reclaimed the house, the Herbers let us revisit it. The presence of the Herbers disturbed me. Looking up at their kitchen table, dodging and darting with their unfamiliar kids, hearing the too-easy talk of the adults, I *knew* that I'd been here before, and I felt as if the Herbers were trespassers.

I felt as if I'd returned from the dead to find my room occupied, my life forgotten. It was a feeling I'd re-experience every time I returned to clean an apartment I'd vacated: the relentless forgetfulness of places.

* * *

Then, a few weeks later, we left our house in town, heading north on the two-lane county road that passed the Lehnertzes' and the Speltzes' places and their staring cows. Then we turned west and chugged up the hill, threading the inside of Devil's Curve, passing the Herbers' new house on the right. But we were not looking at the Herbers' new house. To our left, at the end of the harvested fields, was our farmstead, the highest point in Winona County. The house was obscured by the apple orchard, a mound just big enough for sledding, a walnut tree, the corner of the machine shed and blue spruce trees. But my eyes naturally sought the house.

To the west, tall pines and lilac bushes had been organized into a windbreak. Beyond the windbreak were more fields. As Dad parked the car, we glimpsed the barn at the end of the driveway, and beyond that, the pasture fell away. If I got out of the car and ran around, I would have noticed that the apple orchard was bumpy with fallen fruit and that the soil in the windbreak was dry and shadowed and scattered with pine needles. This was home. For years, when we reached the summit of the wooded hill, we would see that white, two-story house behind those apple trees and pines. A house is a promise kept, again and again, kept every time you return, and it is there on the horizon; but it is such a subtle promise, you never think about it. We simply felt the pleasure of homecoming.

IN THE YEARS BEFORE I ENTERED the first grade—Rollingstone did not have a kindergarten—I would spend much of the day in the pasture. It was maybe forty acres, which dipped and rose (so it couldn't be cultivated). I was small enough to duck under the electric fence, and when I did, the pasture became a kingdom. I would collect milkweed pods, bits of birch bark, dandelions, kidney-shaped pebbles, crepes of moss with moist dirt clinging to their undersides, glitterings of mica, purple flowers from thistles. The gooseberries resembled the irises of eyes. I would follow the pasture's trails and walk its nibbled, cow pie–punctuated grass.

I would spend entire mornings there. I have heard of people raised by wolves; I sometimes feel that, at least for that small portion of my childhood, I was raised by the little filaments in milkweed pods, disciplined by raspberry bushes, socialized by lichen.

PORTRAIT OF THE ARTIST AS A HISSING TODDLER

SOMETHING ELSE WAS HAPPENING IN THOSE FIRST YEARS. One of my first memories—and perhaps my first thought—was brand awareness. Short as a fire hydrant, waddling through Rollingstone, I marveled at litter and logos—the barbed crowns of Grape Nehi and Squirt bottle caps, the pale imprints of Mallo Cup cards, the discarded cylinders and spears of Orange Push-Ups.

Once while we were living in the house in town, I was eager to get somewhere—probably the creamery next door. I tripped over a ridge in the sidewalk, pitched forward, and shattered my teeth. This happened just as speech would otherwise have become second nature to me. To this day, I don't speak well, and when I hear myself on tape, I cringe at the way words slosh in my mouth, and I can hear, in my hesitations, thoughts sparking and failing in my brain. I also now suspect that when my teeth shattered, language scurried back into my brain and a fissure opened between me and the world. I became slightly untethered.

But my shattered teeth and windy speech had an upside:

I started to seek out printed matter. We weren't a literary family, so what I sought out wasn't even a toddler's idea of literature. To the best of my knowledge, I was read no stories. Mom was too busy; Dad had other problems. Dad bragged about reading only one book in high school—*Huckleberry Finn*—and giving four book reports on it. The only book I remember in the house in those days was the Bible. Because we were Catholics, we didn't read the Bible, trusting the priest to interpret it for us. Ours was as heavy as an anvil.

Outside of litter, the first legible things that beckoned to me were the packages that lined supermarket shelves. As my mom piloted me through National Foods or A&P in Winona, I felt as if I'd encountered a menagerie filled with red and green roosters, friendly tigers, perky rabbits, bears in porkpie hats, impish creatures who devoted their lives to cereal or cookies, reassuring Quakers, serene chefs. As soon as I could recognize words, I realized that print is always fluent.

SOMETIME IN THE SIXTIES. The living room was still nesty with Christmas—with bits of wrapping paper, with the artificial tree decorated with blue lights, with the toys that hadn't yet migrated to my room. The house smelled of hot metal, warmed plastic, and pocketbook cookies. I was intent as a surgeon on my favorite Christmas acquisition, Fright Factory. I had poured two colors of Plastigoop into a mold, warmed it in a "heating unit," and immersed it, hissing, in water. Now, as I pulled loose the face I had created, the skin stretched. The face's skin was discolored, its musculature exposed, its surface stitched. My interest in Fright Factory was more fascination than enthusiasm; something dark swam in that pretend flesh.

FLOWERS, ALCOHOL, INFECTION, AND FLESH

FARMS ARE VIOLENT PLACES: ANIMALS ARE KILLED and castrated; machines regularly maim their operators; hail ravages crops; pigs jostle and chomp; dogs eviscerate gophers; watching a cow calving, you realize even birth is violent. And perhaps no domesticated creature is as violent as a bull. Dad reluctantly bought one when we returned to the farm—even though a few years earlier, he had found the Fabers' hired man, who lived down the road, lying lifeless, his skeleton crushed, his body bruised and drained of blood, a human being leaking like a plum. He had been stomped to death by their bull.

The bull would eventually charge. Dad was plowing near the barnyard, floating above the field on the tractor seat, when the new bull threatened Dennis. Dad saw what was happening, leapt off the tractor onto the plowed ground, and sprinted to help him. Dennis was fine; he scrambled away. But when Dad jumped down from the tractor, the metal bone in his hip thrust into its surrounding soft tissue. It was one of many small jostlings that happen on farms—with their rocky, manure-slicked ground; their nervous herds; their elephant-sized machines—and which, in this case, put Dad back in the hospital.

*

So we spent a lot of time visiting Dad at Saint Mary's Hospital in Rochester. Dad's face would ripen with happiness when we entered. I would sit with Mom and whoever else accompanied us in that room that was both sterile and regal. Sterile because of the white sheets, the chrome rails, the bolted TV, the steel urinal. Regal because my dad sat, graciously, in his raised bed, surrounded by his family in what could be mistaken for leisure. Nurses liked him. He would pretend to hook their legs with his cane. But Dad's jauntiness couldn't quite cover the strangeness of the place. Saint Mary's smelled like flesh, alcohol, infection, and flowers.

I would become bored, and they would set me free. I roamed and loitered. I walked the retreating perspectives of halls. I twitched from distraction to distraction like someone flipping channels. I moved amid flowers and holy water fonts and cheaply printed newsprint guides of what to do in Rochester. I darted across the street to the drug store to buy magazines and sandwiches.

Now that I am an adult, I can begin to appreciate the strain these visits must have put on my mother. Tired from working all day on her feet, taking care of a household with five children, and supervising a dairy farm, she drove the forty miles to Rochester down two-lane roads that dipped and rose through farmland and slowed for a half dozen small towns. The only time I remember my parents fighting was when Dad complained that Mom hadn't visited him enough. Her retort to him was devastatingly simple: "I gave you everything I had."

* * *

While I played and blathered and lived my toddler life, my brother and father worked on a faltering farm, and they were acutely aware of its modesty. Rollingstone did not have class differences in the sense of differences of education and values and experiences, but it did have *status* differences. These were measured by who had the newest tractors, the most silos, the largest farm. We had old implements. Besides the tractors, we had a plow, a disk, a hay wagon, a hay baler, and a manure spreader.

Silage was kept in a feed bin. We never bought a new tractor. We always had a John Deere with an old-fashioned, perforated metal, pelvis-shaped seat. Our farm was small, and we had so few cows that we could name them. On the most prosperous farms, they milked over a hundred cows whom they identified with numbers, and concrete silos were supplemented with soaring blue silos. No one drove past our place to admire the skyline of silos; we collected no green and gold trophies of tractors.

Many of our more prosperous neighbors stored their milk in bulk tanks, which a truck from the creamery would empty every morning. But we still used milk cans, so every day, we hauled the milk into town. (In the first weeks back at the farm, we'd even milked by hand.) The cans were heavy, designed to be lifted by a healthy man, which is why Dennis often loaded and deposited the milk. But sometimes Dad and I did. I groaned and staggered under the cans; Dad winced.

I would hop into the back of the pickup. Out on the road, the jostling speed of the truck thrilled me: the road streamed under me, the air streamed over me, the landscape streamed past, my hair and clothes whipped in the wind. Standing in the open cab, I was vulnerable to bumps, to sliding unsecured containers. I gasped for breath; my stomach tickled. By the time we got to Rollingstone, and the pickup slowed, it would smell of gasoline and grease. We would enter the creamery, with its pale smell of unprocessed milk, and the benediction of the Land O'Lakes Indian maiden above the door and the glass block that made the light watery and beautiful.

Dad would visit his friend Bill Klinger, who owned Klinger's Bar. I loved Klinger's: the metal sash that advertised Squirt pop or some other antique brand on the screen door; the malty smell that hit you as you stepped inside; the way the light entering the windows mimicked the color of beer; the jukebox perky as a robot; the dark wood bar; the sand-weighted tartan ashtrays; the Minnesota Twins' schedules; the gleaming, mantis-shaped, miraculously abundant taps; the brightnesses of neon beer logos and beer logo mirrors and the Hamm's clock that featured a relentlessly full-color photograph of a stream rushing over rocks. Happiness condensed in things. I loved Klinger's.

* * *

And I loved the farm in the way you love vulnerable things.

I had a pet cow whom I would feed Mounds bars and to whom I would recount *The CBS Evening News with Walter Cronkite.* I named the cow Danny, oblivious to the fact that cows are females. (I'd never heard the name Danielle.) I repeated the body counts of soldiers killed in Vietnam to Danny and described the riots in Watts and Detroit and Newark. When Danny, perhaps depressed over the state of the nation, stopped giving milk, she was led into a trailer. I was locked into my room when the trailer drove away, but I rioted anyway and registered my body count of one. I didn't quite get the basic thing every farmer has to get: cattle are not pets.

And yet I yearned to farm. Within the farm was a smaller farm, an homage to the green fields and red barn and tractors that surrounded us. I played with miniature farm equipment with Karl Herber, who lived down the road, in a square of dirt the size of an herb garden between the corncrib and the driveway. I knelt on one side of the mock farm. Karl hunched across from me. We both pushed toy John Deere tractors. His hauled a disk, an implement with little pizza-cutter-like blades that mince the ground. Mine hauled a plow, whose comma-shaped blades sliced and churned the earth. Both tractors gleamed green and yellow against the dustier green of the little hay, oat, and corn fields we planted. We left one rectangle of dirt fallow because it is good practice—it restores the nutrients—and because the scale-model government in our heads paid us to.

Our toy tractors were mute, so we made *putt-putt-putt* sounds for them. Godlike, we grabbed them and lifted them across the landscape. We imitated what men yelled to each other in the fields, lowering our voices, making our language technical and slangy and confident: "Yeah, my new 280's been running pretty good." We had no idea what this meant, if there even was a 280 model, but guys on farms said things like that. Karl and I played like children who admired adults and who couldn't wait to join the world of their fathers.

While I played at my fantasy farm, I helped as much as I could on the actual farm. Feeding the calves meant hoisting and pouring from bags of feed as big as I was, so emptying them felt like trying to lift and pour a sleeping person. I mixed the calves' formula in galvanized buckets with rubber teats at the bottom. As I carried the feed and the milk pails through the shadows in the center of the barn, the emerald eyes of rats peered from inside the walls. While the calves fed, the rats considered me. My pulse announced itself. As soon as the calves' sucking turned to slurping, I sprinted away with the plausibly empty pails.

On the other hand, I enjoyed pulling hay and straw bales apart. The taut twine popped when I cut it, and the bales separated into segments. We fed the hay to the cows and spread the straw in the stanchions to absorb manure. We supplemented the hay with oats and ground corn, which we poured into the feed troughs. I helped clean the barn on Saturdays, pushing the straw and manure first into and then down the gutters with a pitchfork and then shoveling it into the manure spreader, which looked like a paddle-wheel boat that flung a wake of shit. I pumped water into five-gallon pails and hauled them—heavy enough to indent lines in my yellow work gloves and hands—in the chill fall air across the farmyard.

I loved working around the barn, especially on cold afternoons in late fall when dusk came early and my breath crystallized and I could crack the ice on the puddles with my green rubber boots. In the barn, bare light bulbs would illuminate the straw; the stanchions; the jostling, bellowing cows; the milking machines. My brother and sisters laughed as they dropped hay bales from the loft. Our place was like a city: people moved around me without much noticing me, occupied with their luminous tasks. Because a recent study had concluded that cows give more milk when they listen to music, a radio, set on a beam, would play. WDGY, which was then the Twin Cities' Top 40 rock station, would play if my brother selected the channel, a country station if my father did. I smelled the ammonia of piss, raw milk, and dry hay, which was fragrant in ways that straw wasn't. Shit was everywhere: splattered on the barn floor; covering the barnyard, where it was scalloped by hooves, like a second topsoil; land-mining the pasture; scattered like croutons on the fields to fertilize the crops; dropped and dripped in the working end of the driveway. The pig shit smelled even more pungent, and the chicken shit got in your nose like sawdust. It says something about how much I loved these people, this intact and industrious family, that I am nostalgic for the smell of crap.

Even I felt no nostalgia toward the killing of chickens. I felt no connection with the BBs of fear that were their eyes or the clumsy engines of loitering and escape that were their bodies. We held them to a tree stump, hacking their necks with a hatchet until the head detached and slackened like a dropped glove. When their heads dropped away, their bodies began to run—as if, in death, they were trying to get open for the game-winning pass they had missed in life—and ejaculate blood out of their necks across the dirt of the driveway. When they had expended their blood and collapsed, we collected them and soaked them in white-freckled blue pans full of hot water until we could pull their feathers off, and then we eviscerated them, sticking our hands into their body cavities and pulling out everything that was not meat or bone.

There is a point at which chores become farming. I tried driving a tractor twice, sitting up on the high, vulnerable seat, coordinating the release of the clutch and the jabbing of the gearshift. But I never really got the hang of it, and I was, in effect, excused. The decision to not push me to learn farming was an act of kindness, because I wasn't any good at it. I lived on a farm, yet I would never be a farmer. But it was also an act of despair. The family didn't want me to apprentice for a job that wouldn't exist.

By now, Dad had undergone several surgeries, and every surgery is a story. A product designer I would meet in 2000 who had devoted his professional life to building surgical tables would tell me, "There is no such thing as minor surgery."

In this story, the hero is my father. He takes his luggage—which my mother packed—and is driven to the hospital. He walks on crutches or a cane, depending on how bad things have become. He answers questions on forms. He hobbles down the telescoping, fluorescent halls of a hospital. He has made this trip so often that the nurses know him, but this probably both comforts and disturbs him. Perhaps he is as sadly jaunty as a friend of mine who, spending weeks on the road launching a business, would announce as he entered hotel lobbies, "Honey, I'm home."

Dad checks into a room with nothing but a bedside table and a TV. There's a stranger in the other bed. The floors are linoleum. After Dad gets into his bed, a nurse pops up the rails on either side and gives him the call light that connects him to her. Mom unpacks his luggage and kisses him good-bye.

That next morning, Dad wakes up alone. He becomes an object. He is washed, and his body is shaved. He is wheeled—lying flat on his back, the halls of the hospital helplessly streaming by—to the operating room.

The next room is even brighter and cleaner than the rest of the hospital. People in green masks calm him, then speak to their peers as if he weren't there. The story shifts to an even more impersonal third person, which I imagine hardens in him:

"The patient is a forty-five-year-old male. He has an extensive history . . ." On his back, he feels disembodied, but all he can think of is how his body will be sliced. He looks up. He floats and thinks of death. The doctor's masked face enters his field of vision. "We're going to apply the anesthesia now," he explains. A breathing mask clamps onto my dad's face. He inhales, and soon the world disappears.

When Dad returned from the hospital, he displayed the discarded hip socket on the living room bureau beside other sockets from other operations. If you did not know their source, the metal objects on the mantel were beautiful. They shined; they lolled; they were made of the finest stainless steel; they had been made with great care for a serious purpose.

The whole living room was a festival of bad taste. A 3-D diorama of Christ hung on the living room wall. Look at the diorama one way, Christ suffered on the cross. Move your head: Christ ascended into heaven. A beige knitted cozy transformed a brandy bottle into a dog standing on its hind legs with buttons for eyes. Dad loved kitsch with the enthusiasm of a man who had never heard the word *kitsch;* he loved it without even bothering to ante up the toll that irony invariably pays to taste. He sang novelty songs to us: "May the Bird of Paradise Fly Up Your Nose," "Tennessee Bird Walk," stuff like that. He bought an Indian headdress made out of artificially red, yellow, and green feathers and talked my mom into photographing him in it.

Dad cared about style, and this had something to do with his sickness. Fashion covers up wounds; fashion asserts that the self is more than its scars and its sores. Of course, there were the starched shirts. Cuff links winked on his nightstand. When he went into Winona, he wore a tie and often a sport coat. As the sixties expanded the palette available to men, he started buying socks in Day-Glo pastels: lime, salmon. He wore pink shirts under tan sport coats. He scented himself with Old Spice, Hai Karate, or Brut. It wasn't expensive cologne because we didn't have access to those kinds of stores. He disciplined his hair with Brylcreem and his whiskers with Aqua Velva. He smoked cigars, which, as any man who has smoked one knows, are part experience, part accessory, and part fragrance. He was fighting the good fight against nakedness and sickness and entropy.

When Dad was in the hospital, Dennis was left to run the farm. The tractor often broke down. Dennis spent hours in the field trying desperately to fix it, and no neighbor ventured over to help. Would the son of a Speltz or a Kreidemacher have felt so isolated? Probably not. But were men who may not have even seen Dennis struggling and who had their own farms to run obliged to come to our family's aid? Dad's sense of grievance is hard to defend.

But the resentment was real. I am now much closer to my father in age. I understand adult anger—the anger of ongoing frustration, the anger of those not-allowed tantrums, the anger of resentment and politics and agendas. And I know that the source of my anger and the object of my anger are often two different things. When I wake up in the morning and I have a deadline that I am afraid of missing, I have rabid political thoughts until I meet the deadline, even though the task weighing on me has nothing to do with politics, even though I'm writing a brochure for office equipment. I'm not without self-knowledge, but I'm unable to stop this strange, savage refraction. And if my father was like me, his emotional metabolism transformed the fear he felt as he lay alone in his hospital bed into anger, because anger is a more desirable emotion. It is more justice-tinged, more active, more hopeful of change, more muscular and masculine. Anger always feels as if it is just about to accomplish something even though it's largely futile. I'm not going to try and trace the precise fractals of my father's emotions, but I'm not sure that he was really angry at the Luxembourgers who apparently thrived around him, and I'm not even sure that he was really angry. He had reason to feel guilty because, by insisting on farming when he was unable to do the work, he put his son in a desperate situation. Dad also had reason to be scared, not of his neighbors but of the destruction that his accident set in motion and that surgery after surgery couldn't defuse.

When my father was convalescing from hip surgery, our family would gather around my parents' bed and watch happy staccato shows filled with double takes and signature lines. On *Laugh-In,* a bikinied, graffitied Goldie Hawn gyrated to rock music, then stopped to say, "Sock it to me!" On *Get Smart,* Don Adams, an adenoidal parody of an international spy, emerged from rubble and smoke and announced, "Missed it by *that much.*"

Dad wore his purple robe over his underwear. His shins and the incision on his hip were purple, as if he had been permanently bruised. He had an ease with his body that only the extremely fit or the extremely sick are allowed. For whatever small consolation they gave him, he loved salves, unguents, and lotions. He greased his chest and throat with Vicks VapoRub. He would spoon it into a frying pan filled with water, then boil the water and inhale the vapors. It would float in slippery reconfiguring islands in the simmering water. He encouraged us to eat a spoonful now and then.* If I remember correctly (no recordings of his voice survive), he talked like a salesman, with a voice as bright as a merry-go-round.

He cajoled us into rubbing cocoa butter on his feet. The cocoa butter smelled like chocolate but reminded me of hospitals. Maybe because we were farm kids—and had seen, say, a veterinarian thrust his arm into a cow's vagina—we were not bothered by my father's feet: his bunion-contoured toes, his amber nails, the inflamed skin that ringed the calluses. We held plaid-encased heating pads to his back, filled rubber hot water bottles, scratched his back or handed him his back scratcher, a plastic

* This is crazy. Don't do it.

hand on a stick. These attentions reminded me of Christ on Holy Thursday, the shock as the priest removed his shoes.

One afternoon, Colleen and I watched TV with Dad on the bed. The recovery from his surgery—his seventh? his ninth?—was not going well. Dad told us something that I didn't pay much attention to at the time, something that both then and now seems understandable: *One day you will find me hanging from one of the trees in the pasture.* I am amazed how *parenthetical* my father's despair was. Despite his despairing talk, he never surrendered to it. The dominant chord of my childhood was this: All of us were trying as hard as we could. It just wasn't enough.

WHEN I WAS A TODDLER, WORDS proliferated in my mind. But actually speaking was another matter entirely. Speech, in its gnashings and lubrications, its existential insistence and its panicky acknowledgment of the other, seems to have felt as shocking as sex. My speech was so incomprehensible that Mom often could not understand what I was trying to say, which only made me try harder and which made my attempts at words even more opaque with panic. Sometimes Mom and I would just have to wait for Colleen to come home from school. She would squat in front of me and look me in the face, calm me, and somehow decipher what I was saying so that I would not be locked inside myself.

TRANSISTOR RADIOS

FEBRUARY IN MINNESOTA IS DISMAL, EVEN IF YOUR FARM isn't struggling and your father isn't damaged. And in February of 1964, President Kennedy had been dead only three months. Contemporary accounts—such as John Updike's 1963 Christmas "Talk of the Town" piece in the *New Yorker*—describe an especially overcast time. The popular music was thin, warbly, and chaste. "Dominique" by the Singing Nun had topped the charts in December. It was actually sexier than "There! I've Said It Again" by Bobby Vinton, which was number one throughout January.

We heard that WLS in Chicago was going to play the first song by a new group. We had set a transistor radio on the kitchen counter. My brother and sisters pushed the kitchen table and chairs aside to create a dance floor. They turned the volume up.

"I Want to Hold Your Hand" didn't play so much as it exploded; it incited; it abraded. It began with a guitar riff—tinny to modern ears—that repeated as if rallying support. The vocal, pushed along by hand claps, rose into a falsetto. John Lennon fought out of the song's syrupy break—*It's such a feeling that my love*—by singing the next phrase—*I can't hide, I can't hide, I can't hide*—so adamantly that his voice almost gave out. Everybody danced—Maureen with Dennis, Colleen with Sheila, me presumably careening by myself. We thought without thinking.

The phrase "this changes everything" now means almost nothing, thanks to the lazy bravado of some advertising that will have us believe that a new razor blade or midsized sedan will transform the world. But that goofy little single really did change everything or at least everything that a pop song could change. It didn't rewrite physics or discover a new continent, but it did unleash a vast energy—an energy that you could feel in your bones, that felt both subversive and sweet, that was multiplied by a million radios, and that transformed an assassination-dulled and February-blighted population into so many puppies. Maybe it was all demographics and hormones, nothing more than, in Keith Richards's phrase, turning on sixteen-year-old girls. But this felt different.

I despair of making the impact of the Beatles clear. People even a few years younger than me listen to the early songs and hear only a boy band. Yes, "I Want to Hold Your Hand" was about the single most innocent erotic act. Yet the music knew what the words wouldn't say. The song's image was dopey but its subject was human yearning. Lock yourself in a closet and listen to Bobby Vinton's "There! I've Said It Again" for a few hours and picture a world in which that was the high point. Then listen to "I Want to Hold Your Hand."

How much else did we know about this song and its creators? Had we seen them on Sullivan yet? Had we seen them move girls to scream and faint? Had we seen the interview where John, when asked how he found America, replied, "Turn left at Greenland"? Did we know that they wrote their own songs? That they admired the music of Negroes and sharecroppers? That they were, themselves, working class?

Were we working class? The question's tricky in America. My mom had graduated from college, and Dad nominally owned the farm. But we considered ourselves working class. Nurses and farmers work around shit. We had little money. One of the few Bible verses my mom quoted insisted that "it is easier for a camel to go through the eye of a needle than for a rich man to enter the kingdom of God." The Beatles were working-class boys who wrote their own songs. Somehow, I noted that. I turned toward these working-class boys who made songs, like a plant turning toward the sun.

I wasn't alone. The Beatles and their peers thrived in our house. We played records *constantly*—in the girls' room but also on the console stereo in the living room. We didn't just play the records; we danced to them. In the house of a man who struggled to walk, movement was a sacrament.

* * *

The new electric music was everywhere. When we came in from chores, Petula Clark's "Downtown" whispered the romance of cities into our lives. In a voice both glossy and soothing, still accented, Clark conjured images of bright taxi cabs in granite canyons; of rain that saturated the air like harmony and neon that inflected the air like melody; of hurried, purposeful, joyful movement; of blossoming umbrellas; of incandescent windows and incendiary clubs. Sheila and I loved it.

* * *

I looked forward to learning to read because reading promised liberation from my breathy, straining speech. And when I started first grade at Holy Trinity School, I immediately liked its crowded energy, its momentum and clamor: boys stampeding down stairs, girls gathering and dispersing in chatty groups. I inhaled the distinctive Pine-Sol smell; my feet deepened the light half moons in the same steps my mother and now my brother and sisters climbed; I touched the sponge in the holy water font in the hallway; I looked up at the cloudy blackboards, at the green institutional paint, and at the crucifixes—the pierced, half-naked, heaven-supplicating Christ. The trip to Holy Trinity was my first commute. I awoke, prepared myself, left home with routine urgency, traveled, felt the subtle indifferences and brightnesses and adrenalines of a place where things are accomplished. School was a brisk promise.

But reading initially disappointed me. The nuns—like teachers everywhere at the time—taught reading through phonics. The phonics method assumed that children were comfortable with speech and taught them to read by breaking words down into sounds. And, in the case of the vast majority of children, this approach reassured them. But phonics disappointed me. When I saw *o* and *a* on the printed page, they were crisp, confident things; when I said them, they smooshed into "uhh." Words invigorated me, but sounds baffled me. It was as if I had been told to dance the syllables. Other kids struggled with real disabilities, but I didn't notice. Phonics enforced an averageness upon me that I hated.

I found in sports the fluency I was looking for in school. I added commentary tracks to everything my friend Karl Herber and I did, including sports. Maybe all kids did this, but for me, experience was always distilled to story and sharpened to style, and probably not in an entirely healthy way. When you confuse the box score with the game, you miss things.

Standing in the yard, I assumed a batting stance, my bat twitching behind me, my head facing forward, my feet planted. Because we couldn't yet connect with the baffling butterfly of a thrown pitch, Karl rolled a softball on the ground toward me. I announced, with an ease I only achieved while playing with friends, "Fenton smacks a hot grounder back to the pitcher, ending the inning." While we couldn't hit a tossed ball, we could sometimes catch one. When Karl stabbed one of my floating throws out of the air with his glove, I'd improvise, "Herber nabs it," and then I would instruct him, "and spins and fires it home to Fenton, catching the runner at the plate."

While the possibility of being injured by machinery or animals kept farm talk sober, sports talk could intensify into joy. I bounce the basketball twice and deke my hip sideways a little. I squint, get two hands beneath the ball, push it outward and upward like a swimmer doing the breaststroke, and arc the shot up from less than ten feet out toward the orange hoop that Dennis had nailed to our barn. The ball climbs toward the basket. It wobbles in midflight. It touches the backboard and, too exhausted to do much else, collapses through the hoop. "Yes! Fenton wins it at the buzzer!" Stories emerged from my blathering.

* * *

Dennis and I slept in a bedroom, but I otherwise claimed it as a kind of personal retreat. In my room, I listened to sports. Pine tree branches scraped against the window when the wind blew. The green-blue walls tilted inward with the rooflines. Eight-by-ten glossies of Tony Oliva and Bob Allison and Harmon Killebrew, collected at National Foods, smiled from the walls. The voice of Herb Carneal, the Twins announcer, emerged from the radio. Through holes in the radio's back, I could see the glowing tubes. The sky was still light but getting dark. My room felt like a tree house, both open and safe. Everyone else watched TV downstairs.

I sat on the bed as if on a raft at sea while the Twins game unfolded. I dealt myself my baseball cards—the Twins and then their opponent. I stared at these talismans; I read the little paragraphs on their backs. If the game got too close and the excitement too much, I sometimes shut off the radio.

Or it was winter, same scene, but the windows were already glossy with darkness, reflecting my decorated walls, and I listened to the North Stars hockey game. The announcer narrated as quickly as he could, but he barely kept up with the action. How did the players move so quickly? Pass so deftly? Apparitions named Parise and Grant and Maniago and Goldsworthy performed acrobatics. I came to hockey as a blind man; I heard it before I saw it. I came to hockey as I come to a novel now; some-one else's words prompted my own pictures.

At such moments, with the transistor tubes glowing and the dark windows shining, my room felt like a tree house. If I could, I would have pulled up the ladder that connected this tree house to the world.

DENNIS LOVED BASKETBALL. He once walked three miles down the wooded hill at the edge of our fields in a snowstorm to practice. And my parents attended every Holy Trinity game, both home and away, traveling skinny and treacherous roads in winter to little towns forty miles distant, the trees on the side of the road encroaching like monsters. The whole family attended every home game. Even as played by Class C farm boys, basketball still had all its essential charms—the texture of the game itself, as sweaty as a locker room and as bright as a stage; the echoing, agitated crowd; the trembling bleachers; the controversies of fouls; the recital-like isolation of free throws; the mathematical otherworldliness of a perfectly arced shot; the zephyrlike exhilaration of fast breaks. Dennis was gifted and gutty, often double-teamed, and we cheered for him and agonized with him and became indignant at bad calls, and the cheering really did seem an expression of love.

THE TEENAGERS ARE WINNING

RIGHT AROUND THE TIME I WAS STARTING SCHOOL, VATican II softened the stony intolerance of fifties Catholicism, the Catholicism that viewed itself as "the old faith . . . at war with the new paganism." The council's primary document is remarkable, addressing "all who invoke the name of Christ" and "the whole of humanity." Variants on *human* and *mankind* appear twenty times in a five-paragraph preface. More tellingly, its verbs tremble with humanity. The council that drafted it "yearns to explain" how it "conceives of the . . . Church in the world of today." It invokes its "respect and love for the entire human family with which it is bound up" and finds that faith demands "engaging [with non-Catholic humanity] in a conversation."

As a result of this document,* Holy Trinity stopped celebrating the Mass in Latin and started celebrating it in English—not the

*The document I'm quoting is popularly known as Vatican II but known officially as *The Pastoral Constitution on the Church in the Modern World,* Gaudium Et Spes, *Promulgated By His Holiness Pope Paul VI On December 7, 1965.* I did not read it until 2004.

true vernacular of used car ads and pop songs and barnyards, but its plangent cousin. "From age to age you gather a people to yourself so that from east to west a perfect offering may be made to the glory of your name." While my brother and sister each took their First Communion with their class in a radiant giggling herd, I tasted the Communion host—which seemed more parchment than bread as it dissolved in my mouth—alone, stage-dazzled, in my little sport coat. The idea was that the sacraments were a *personal* discovery of God, so everyone in my class had to take First Communion on a different Sunday. Although they generally approved of Vatican II, my parents thought this nod to personal preferences a little too close to Protestantism. It didn't last.

As a result of the reforms of Vatican II, Sister Maureen would strum "They Will Know We Are Christians by Our Love," sitting on the grass, her bare knees exposed. The effect was humanizing rather than sexualizing. Sister Maureen talked about going to the movies and, as a girl, going to Cubs games in her native Chicago.

Sister Maureen taught us religion that year because Sister Azaria wasn't expected to be up to the new theology. We did not see Sister Azaria's knees. She had been a nun for untold decades, and she continued to wear her floor-length habit. She was, literally, old school.

Old-school Catholicism contained kindness as well as harshness. Once when Sister Azaria was leading the whole throng of us second graders up from recess, I was following closely behind her. At the top of the stairs, I stumbled forward and stepped on the hem of her habit, flipping her backward down the stairs, spilling and scattering eight-year-olds. Her leg broke. In the chaos, it wasn't clear what exactly caused her fall. She never told anyone that I tripped her.

Sister Azaria kept my secret. I developed no guilt about this incident, even though the term most associated with Catholicism in the memories of others is *guilt*. Perhaps because of the graciousness of the nuns I encountered in Rollingstone, I never developed Catholic guilt—which is actually a kind of Catholic shame—at all.

*

The thaw of Vatican II took more interesting forms with the high school kids.

Catholic schools are portrayed in works such as Christopher Durang's *Sister Mary Ignatius Explains It All for You* as comic tyrannies where students are brutalized by nuns tough as linebackers and nimble as fencers. These monsters dispelled any rebellion with a smack of the metal-edged ruler.

This wasn't my experience. By the mid-sixties, the teenagers were on the verge of winning. Shows like *Where the Action Is, Hullabaloo,* and *American Bandstand* transformed teenagers into mythical creatures, not actual human beings but prototypes of some future, better, sleeker human. The Beatles were winning. *Laugh-In* was winning. Twister was winning.

Maureen had started sneaking up behind male teachers, and even priests, and murmuring in a mannish voice, "Hey, baby," prompting them to spin their heads only to discover a teenage girl.

Dennis and some of his friends put baby roosters in the drawers of the chemistry room. (The roosters were thrown alive into trash cans by the chick hatchery because they were useless for egg-laying.) Sister Eileen could hear that something was wrong, but her hearing wasn't good enough to locate the birds. So the desks continued to chirp throughout class.

Sister Eileen, who was slipping into senility and deafness, had everyone give a report each month on something they read in a magazine. Dennis's friend Carlus Dingfelder gave his report on a "cow of the future" that was constructed of plastic. You put hay and certain digestive chemicals in it, and it produced milk. Sister said, "I've never heard about this, Carlus. What magazine did you find it in?"

"Cow Monthly."

"Cow Monthly?"

"It's a special magazine. You have to be a farmer to get it," Carlus deadpanned. The class exploded with laughter. Sister, baffled, beaten, let Carlus finish his report.

*

These were normal teenage pranks, but the spirit of the times suffused and elevated each individual incident. What's vandalism in one age is rebellion in another. There's not that much distance between *Animal House* and Woodstock.

The times suffused the town. Sister Maureen asked me to bring in Simon and Garfunkel's "The Sound of Silence" so that she could play it for the junior high religion class. The song is a catalog of generational self-infatuation: the boy-I'm-sensitive guitar of the intro; the recreational depression of "Hello darkness, my old friend,/I've come to talk with you again"; the groovy ennui of "People talking without speaking,/People hearing without listening"; the Jesus-in-the-temple storminess of "And the people bowed and prayed/To the neon God they made"; the photogenic suffering of "I turned my collar to the cold and damp." Whereas older generations of nuns would speak to the sinfulness of their students, Sister Maureen spoke to their alienation.

This is the cultural context in which my brother challenged the qualifications of a priest to teach the class on marriage. And this is the context in which the priest said, "Well, Mr. Fenton, if you know so much, why don't you teach it yourself?" And Dennis did. It may say even more about the times—and the affection with which Dennis was regarded in Rollingstone—that no one remembers any fallout from this. Ten years earlier, Dennis's stunt would have been heresy.

On Saturday nights, we said the rosary, but the older kids said it like horses restrained at the gates. Mom and Dad prayed from the bedroom. Colleen, kneeling next to me on the couch, snickered provocations under her breath. The Saturday rosary celebrates five joyful mysteries, the last of which was the finding of Jesus in the temple. Joseph and Mary forget Jesus and rush back, panicked, to find their child. The mystery ends, "Mary keeps all these things in her heart." When the last joyful mystery was concluded and the last "Our Father" was said, the other children rushed to a movie in Winona or a dance in the neighboring farm town of Lewiston. There, a band named J. C. and the Apostles covered Beatles and Kinks songs. We didn't see any contradiction in rosaries followed by rock and roll. Even my parents would sometimes go out. There were the rogue priests who condemned dancing, but that was more personal strangeness than church doctrine. My mom liked to point out that Jesus's first miracle was changing water to wine at a celebration. Jesus brought the keg.

On Sunday night, we made Chef Boy-ar-dee pizza, and the cheery primary colors of the sixties blazed in the kitchen: the mix in a bright yellow box, prepared in a bright yellow bowl. Pepsi fizzed like a discotheque. We greased pans with margarine that gooshed between our fingers, poured water into the flour to create a bland dough that we pushed and furrowed into the pan, then covered it with tomato sauce and cheese from a can and burdened it with browned hamburger. The pan ticked in the oven. The kitchen warmed. Dennis and the girls taunted each other with talk that felt like the bubbles rising and rioting in pop.

That energy also fizzed in the music that was always on in our house, in the TV shows we loved, in Maureen singing "The Lion Sleeps Tonight," in manic games of kickball and Twister, in summer rides along our field roads in our pickup when Maureen would drive and the rest of us would sit in the back, taking turns sitting on the tailgate, the dirt and grass streaming below us like rapids, our stomachs lightening and tickling. We leaned forward and raised our hands so that if the pickup hit a bump, we would spill off the truck.

Sometimes the baby pigs would get out at night and squirt through the air with the desperation of something that craves freedom. Sleep-dazed, in the moonlight, our whole family pursued an entire field of sentient, squirming footballs. I think we secretly rooted for the pigs. They were the teenagers of the farmyard—out too late, moving too fast, giddy and fierce. Like the Dave Clark Five, our pigs were "young with all of their might."

APPRAISING SOME FRESHLY opened baseball cards, I realized I now had two Manny Motas, and so, for the first time, I approached the phone hanging from our kitchen wall. I had seen everyone else in the family use this intimate machine. I detached the receiver and pressed it to my ear and mouth. It was a party line, so I listened for other talkers. I'd written John Kendrick's number down after looking it up in our skinny phone book. I placed my finger in the six hole in the dial, rotated it, and felt a small centrifugal tug and then a small satisfaction when I released the dial and that digit registered. I dialed six more numbers. An abyss of silence waited at my ear. The phone rang with a mechanical boorishness. A voice—a person stripped of face and gesture—answered. The chaos of the Kendricks' house rampaged behind the silence. John came to the phone. The words are lost to me, but I know we transacted our business and that he was glad to hear from me. We agreed to exchange baseball cards the next day. The world had enlarged a little, which prompted my usual mix of optimism and neurosis. For the rest of my life, I'd view phones as part can-do appliance, part interpersonal abyss.

INSIDE OTHER HOMES

I STARTED TO BETTER UNDERSTAND MY HOME—AND WHAT a happy place my parents had created—by visiting other homes. To the unfortunate parents hosting them, overnights look like anarchy, but when I was a kid, they felt like anthropology. The Kendricks' house made our house seem sedate. Mr. Kendrick—a professor at Saint Mary's College in Winona—had died when John was five, leaving Mrs. Kendrick with fourteen children and a culture of eccentricity. When alive, Mr. Kendrick didn't allow a TV in the house. He didn't own a car but instead hitchhiked seven miles into work every day. The entire family walked to church, and Mr. Kendrick lined everyone up—the boys in their little suits, the girls in their Sunday dresses—for inspection before they entered the church. If there were no altar boys, Mr. Kendrick—a *grown man,* as the italics of gossip would later put it—would vault the communion rail and serve as an altar boy. He vaulted the rail, I presume, because Christ had said that we must become as children to enter his kingdom. As his own brother wrote him in the 1940s in letters discovered by his son Tom, "You have too many modern ideas, Clyde Kendrick." Widowed,

Mrs. Kendrick flight-controlled the family as best she could. She bought a VW van.

When I visited John, we did not play cowboys and Indians but simply Indians. "Playing Indian" meant taking hikes, searching for arrowheads by Bear Creek, stalking animals and identifying plants, and arguing about the practices of various tribes. The Kendrick boys played mock war games and "counted coup," which, as John explained, is how Indians gained recognition in battle. I joined in, not because I had any political conviction—I also admired Pete Maus's cowboy regalia—but because it was fun, because a society based on constant camping and skirmishing wars seemed too good to be true. Sometimes the war games would become violent. John and his brothers Tom and Joe would wrestle with a ferocity that I had never experienced before. For them, wrestling was a form of grief. At the Kendricks', I felt for the first time the anxious, amputated feeling of a fatherless house.

Sports begat more friendships and introduced me to more families. When I stayed overnight at Jerry Kreidemacher's, I shot pool with Jerry and his brothers. They viewed pool as a version of hockey. They checked, elbowed, and skirmished. They crowded around the table and taunted whoever was shooting to ruin the shooter's concentration and test his mettle. The Kreidemachers were rough but generous, perfect brothers. When I admired a collection of *Sport* magazines from the fifties that an uncle had collected, Jerry checked with his parents and then just gave them to me. So I took home the particular sweet smell of aged magazine paper, the milky color photographs of the fifties, and the breathlessly earnest advertisements for Brylcreem and aftershave. I felt nostalgia for the first time. For me, nostalgia was not return—I had not lived through the years cataloged—but a fragrant simplification of life.

*

When I stayed at other friends' houses, even my oblivious young self noticed something: the atmosphere was a little more Prussian and Puritan, the rules were a little more explicit, the atmosphere a little more tense. Nobody was going to be spontaneously dancing to the Beatles in the kitchen. I experienced nothing dysfunctional—I would know true dysfunction in a few years and recognize it immediately. In fact, what I saw was the discipline and standards I still pretty much believe will save America if only they prevailed in every household. But when one of my little friends screwed up and was getting yelled at, I didn't know where to look or what to do. I stared at the varnish on the woodwork. The fact that I didn't get yelled at made it worse. My eyes sought the neutrality of furniture, wainscoting, banisters, wallpaper, and trim. But when you feel this uneasy, the room absorbs your anxiety—the woodwork squirmed, the patterns on the wallpaper fidgeted (in a way I would later recognize in Bergman movies).

I couldn't wait to get home, where I could breathe again, where my sisters might be dancing to "Palisades Park," where Dennis—in a rare moment of relaxation—might be roaring laughter at some sitcom, where Dad might be singing "May the Bird of Paradise Fly Up Your Nose." I now realize that my parents didn't just tolerate all this fun; they helped create it. Our fun was a version of their raucous games of cards with Uncle John and Aunt Margaret, of their evenings out with Hudsy and Sylvia Hengel, of their happy visits to Klinger's Bar. Underneath the fun was the purity of my mother's Christianity. If you treated people with love and you kept your promises, you were a good person. Period. You didn't need to get As; you didn't need to be the most prosperous farmer; you didn't need to make the varsity team. I don't mean to whitewash my parents' characters—Dad's stubbornness could be viewed as selfishness; their financial decisions might not bear scrutiny; in later years, Mom would become theologically severe—but I cannot escape my sense of gratefulness.

And there was something else special about the home they had created. While I had a great time on my overnights, and while I had sampled what a life jostling with brothers would be like (Dennis really functioned like an uncle in my life), I realized something I couldn't articulate for decades: I always wanted to return to the house I saw as I ascended the hill and emerged from the woods at the highest point in Winona County. It was, among other things, a place of solitude, an artists' retreat for one ten-year-old.

OUR TV WAS THE EIGHTH member of our family. I could not imagine a life without the daffiness of Lisa and the doltishness of Eb on Green Acres, *without the camp assurances and boarding school diction of* Batman *("Don't worry, old chum; we shall vanquish these ne'er-do-wells if it is the last thing we do!"), without the verbal popcorn of* Laugh-In, *without the squinting bafflement of Don Adams on* Get Smart, *without the good sense of Kate and the grumbling of Uncle Joe on* Petticoat Junction, *without the histrionics of Kirk and the serenity of Spock on* Star Trek.

Dennis, Maureen, Sheila, and Colleen

DINOSAURS AND SPIROGRAPHS

ONE SATURDAY, MOM BROUGHT HOME WITH THE GROCERies a folio titled *Wonders of the Animal Kingdom.* Its illustrated cover teemed with all sorts of incompatible wildlife; inside pages were divided into empty rectangles that awaited stamps. That first Saturday, a packet of dinosaur stamps also spilled onto the kitchen table. It was as if Mom had brought home a pet.

I licked the dinosaur stamps, affixed them to their designated spaces in the book, and read the captions below them. The dinosaurs fascinated me: their hostile skins and toothy spines, the way they combined the thrill of science fiction with the thrill of the murdered. The story of the earth became a series of drafts, an Etch A Sketch that could be redone. Children are natural evolutionists—or, if there is such a thing, iterationists. They know man isn't the only magic trick God can perform. Two weeks later, as if to confirm the wonder of creation, a packet of fish—some spiked, some candy-colored, some bloated as bagpipes—plopped onto the kitchen table. I came to like the taste of the glue on the stamps, which reminded me of the taste of dissolving Communion hosts.

At this same time, thanks to a convincing salesman, the red bindings of the *Encyclopedia Britannica Junior* brightened what had been an almost empty family bookcase. The red junior version beckoned like a city of knowledge, and its plastic smells released a modern happiness in my brain.

Then, on a late February afternoon not unlike the ones when we first encountered the Beatles, my parents presented me with a birthday present: a Spirograph. When the box opened, clear plastic gears fell out: circles, toothed hollow rings, oblongs with rounded edges. The kit also included four colored pens and a guidebook showing the snowflakelike designs you could create. By placing a colored pen in a given hole in a given wheel and rotating it within a given ring, you created a pattern. Place another pen in another hole and complicate the pattern. As I moved the pen in the gear, orbits appeared on the paper.

This was not self-expression—there were no flourishes suffused with pain, no joyous doodles. This mechanization was fine with me; my self-expressions were ugly—my speech sloshed in my mouth; my handwriting and drawing jerked across the page.

Spirograph caused me to see design elsewhere. Sitting in my room on a spring night after school, I examined a pack of 1967 baseball cards recently liberated from their wrapper and still smelling of the powdered sugar that dusted the accompanying gum. Baseball cards freeze the players so they can be contemplated. Many of the cards were face shots; some were action poses. Sky and fields showed behind the players. Their team name—Astros, Cubs, Tigers—anchored the bottom of the card in confident, colored letters: mauve, sienna, magenta, yellow, green, red. Yes, these men played a game I loved. But there was something else in my love of baseball cards. Kerning, leading, color theory, layout: I did not know these disciplines existed, but I loved what happened inside of me when I saw ink that had been thoughtfully guided onto paper.

*

One Saturday afternoon in May, when I turned on the TV, the screen pulsed and a grey diamond appeared. Curt Gowdy's tobacco-leaf voice explained that a game was about to begin. A pitcher tossed warm-ups; a crowd accumulated in the bleachers in Baltimore or Boston. I had discovered the NBC *Game of the Week.* A whole literature celebrates the pastoral pleasures of baseball. But the ancestral home of the game I watched on this Saturday was no pasture: it was 1920s New York, where the Yankees fielded a lineup called Murderer's Row and started a pitcher actually named Urban Shocker. The colors were grey; the patterns, geometric; the actions, ballistic. Here on TV, the improvised bases of our backyard games were standardized into chalk-described lines. Typography graced the uniforms. The ball was hard, the pitches accurate, the cleats real, the velocities and vectors dangerous, the choreography demanding: a fastball was brutally redirected into a home run, a ground ball was crisply transformed into a double play. Baseball was ballet improved by the threat of violence. Like Spirograph, baseball enacted designs within designs.

As I watched game after game, the broadcasts gathered around them everything that was good about Saturday afternoon—the often-blue skies, the pine trees by the windows, the absolute vacation of those hours in late May and September with no school or church obligations, the excitement of a Saturday in summer. When he was well, Dad was around. He held onto a boyhood bias for the White Sox, so he would mock the Twins, but we both liked the *Game of the Week.*

And the thread that gathered all this was Curt Gowdy's voice. Like all baseball announcing, his voice was an art within an art. He gave backstory and highlighted challenges and paid compliments and, pitch by pitch, created the story of the game, and the story of the game became the game. When I saw an ad in *Sport* magazine showing Gowdy and two college-age aspiring announcers, illustrated, in a press box, a cloudlike distance above the field, I articulated my first ambition: I wanted to be a sports announcer. The fact that talking on the phone freaked me out and that I spoke so poorly my own mother couldn't understand didn't seem to matter to me. What's even more touching is that it didn't seem to matter much to the adults I announced my plans to. Of course, you have to be a special kind of jerk to mock an eight-year-old's ambition. And on a deeper level, I had identified my vocation: I wanted to be to the world what Curt Gowdy was to baseball. I wanted to tell stories and comment on life. I wouldn't be able to articulate that for years, but I first noticed the power of words listening to Curt Gowdy. An announcer creates the memoir of the moment.

MY ELDEST SISTER, MAUREEN, spent evenings in summer sitting on the swing that hung between two evergreen trees on the far edge of our front yard. It was a wooden swing, painted red and white, wide enough for two. Its movement calmed and connected you, like immersion in water. The swing looked out over the county road and the Herbers' fields. Maureen would listen to the radio for hours as the sun, off to her left, didn't so much set as ripen. Over the course of an evening, only one or two cars would disturb her meditation. I now suspect that, in her soft way, she was leaving home.

THE TEENAGERS ARE LOSING

ON DECEMBER 22, 1966, THE *WINONA DAILY NEWS* REPORTED that Holy Trinity School would close. The diocese believed that "there is no possibility of giving the kind of terminal education necessary for people not going to college—agriculture, welding shop, auto mechanics, etc. that some students would find necessary to go into the farming community around Rollingstone."

Monsignor Habiger, the diocese's superintendent of schools, continued, "Nor can we present the many courses for the college-bound student, for instance in the field of physics and chemistry."

The superintendent then added this illiteracy: "The expanding economy of America in terms of the Gross National Product is going to demand a sophisticated people beyond which we have not experienced." Were the sensible farmers I knew really snowed by this talk about their children and the future? Maybe. What parents don't want to prepare their child to be one of the "sophisticated people" who thrives in an "expanding economy"? This was, after all, the era of the Space Race, and everyone's head was filled with visions of a curvilinear future with treadmills in the sky and flying cars. (No one ever imagined flying tractors because they would be a contradiction in terms; tractors are rooted machines.)

But the diocese was also set on shutting off its support. Whatever the reason, the attendees at the meeting voted overwhelmingly to close the school.

One of the gifts of writing memoir is a calm that comes from finally seeing other people's side of the story. And for me, anger is often a complicated, dishonest emotion: I say that I want to change the world, but what I enjoy is the private pleasure of self-righteousness. But forty years later, the manipulation in Habiger's statements still makes me angry. The notion that farm boys who had apprenticed beside their fathers for a dozen years needed a class in agriculture to farm is ridiculous. The privileging of technology over teaching (and the overstatement of technology's importance in the teaching of science) is philistine. And the almost mystical invocation of a "more sophisticated" future is bullshit. Habiger's speech exuded the condescension that administrators so often feel toward those they serve. There's a disingenuousness here that's far more cynical than mere lying.

The diocese's decision didn't make only me angry. I spoke with Sister Conrad, who had been the principal of the school up until 1965 and who in 2004 was eighty and living in the mother superior home in Rochester. She had asked to be transferred a year before the school closed. She would not be the one to close it because—and she would be in a position to know—there was still support for the school.

Dennis's class would be the last to graduate. Grades seven through twelve would finish the year and then be discontinued; the kids on the ridge would be bussed to Lewiston High School, the kids in the valley to Winona High School. Holy Trinity Elementary School would remain open for two more years and then become a public school.

* * *

I retreated into books and pop culture. But while I loved words and images, I distrusted plot. I walked out of the room when the TV became too suspenseful, when Captain Kirk was trapped beneath the surface of an alien world, when the Twins' pitcher was embattled in the ninth inning and the opponent's slugger loomed at the plate. But the plots I hated most of all were those of *I Love Lucy.* As soon as I heard the brassy, space-age, whistling-in-the-dark of the opening credits, I extinguished the show however I could—by switching off the set, by looking away if I was at a friend's house, by retreating to my room.

In my dislike of *I Love Lucy,* I was on to something. I recently forced myself to watch an episode. Ricky has challenged Lucy to work out of the home for a week. Cut to a factory scene: an anonymous, silent, scowling, but competent woman is topping gliding candies with chocolate. Lucy tries to mimic her coworker, slops too much chocolate onto her workspace, daubs at it nervously, and drenches a piece of candy, which drools chocolate as she sets it aside. Now that Lucy's hands are muddied with chocolate, her nose itches. She twitches and shakes her head and asks her coworker what she does in such a situation. Her competent coworker remains as silent as machinery. A fly buzzes. Lucy looks around to locate the buzzing. She senses it behind her. She darts her head. The fly settles on her coworker. Lucy slaps her with chocolate. And it is in this moment that I would have to look away because I know what happens next—the flurry of violence. Just as I would have to look away later when Ricky, who has become a housewife for a week, boils four pounds of rice, which cascades down the front of the stove. And I would have to look away when the assembly line carrying the candies accelerates and Lucy can't wrap them, so she stuffs them into her mouth and down her dress and the door opens and the supervisor . . .

What I felt but did not think was *there were enough accidents already.* There were enough machines creating enough damage. There were enough incisions and enough unconsciousness. Every surgery is slapstick, a remarkable violence that pretends to normalcy. As an adult fiction writer and teacher, I would have to work hard to learn plot because I'd run from the room whenever it appeared in my youth. As an adult reader, I would have to learn how to enjoy the thrill of story and suspense.

Mom was the anti-Lucy. As Dad got sicker, she had to work even harder and move even faster. She was always practical, capable, and adamant. It radiates from the picture of her and Dad holding their babies. Her face is serious, pale—an Irish face, white skin surrounded by black hair—looking down at Dennis in such a way that she seems sleepy-lidded. She worked forty hours a week as an obstetrics nurse, which meant both morning shifts and night shifts, which meant standing for eight hours, which meant attending difficult deliveries and premature births and witnessing the occasional death of a baby. (She would sometimes, covertly, baptize dying babies so they would go to radiant heaven rather than watery limbo.) The stress on her legs from nursing gave her varicose veins. She had only recently learned to drive, and to get to work, she would navigate our sharp-cornered hill in winter. She woke up at five in the morning, made cocoa, made toast, woke us, and served us. With help from my sisters, she cooked and cleaned and performed the other duties of a farm wife—shopping, canning vegetables, baking fist-sized cinnamon rolls, gutting and cleaning chickens. She attended church every Sunday and holy day. She attended school events—games, plays, and fairs. When my father was in the hospital, she saw to it that Dennis and the girls ran the farm. Her diabetic mother lived alone; Mom would drive to Rollingstone and then head back west to give her insulin. Her life was a desperate to-do list, a Möbius strip of tasks.

I imagine Mom rushing through the day, distracted and refocusing on the next thing she had to do. She was dehydrated because she drank coffee, not water. She was oxygen-starved because she couldn't stop for long enough to take a deep enough breath. Her feet ached because she carried 130 pounds on them for hours. Her eyes twitched because she drove over farm roads for forty miles through the dark to see her husband in the hospital and then back through the dark.

She drank seventeen cups of coffee a day.

When we returned for third grade, school was ghostly. A year earlier, we had heard the storming of the older kids over our heads in the labs and classrooms upstairs. But now, with the junior high and high school gone, it was quiet. It is hard to pick up a silence in the monkey asylum of a grade school, but it was there. And we also missed the charisma of teenagers, who were never more celebrated than they were in the sixties and who, to the second-grader sensibility, thundered around us like gods. The empty rooms on the third floor and the quiet halls and the depopulated lunchroom reminded us that schools are less closed than amputated.

With the high school gone, grown-ups had fewer reasons to come into town. There would be no more basketball games, Latin fairs (where high school students did projects based on their Latin class), school plays, and graduations. The glue of gossip evaporated.

Why didn't parents send their kids to Cotter, the Winona Catholic high school? Eventually some did. The Kendricks did right away. But Holy Trinity was not a private school in the sense that Cotter was. It was more like what would now be a charter school. It charged no tuition to individual families. Rather, it was funded by the contributions of the whole town to the parish and supplemented by a stipend from the diocese. In a town where some families had nine children in school in any given year, the new private tuitions were prohibitive. But parents may still have doubted their own faith when they decided to not send their kids to Catholic schools. A classmate of Sheila put it more bluntly, forty years later: the town gave up.

Colleen and Sheila went to Lewiston, which we'd demonized as a country and western song, a place of Protestantism, of irregular churchgoing, of adultery, of divorce. The truth was somewhat less dramatic. Colleen found the farm boys to be entertaining while Sheila thought they teased her. While Lewiston wasn't Sodom, it also wasn't Holy Trinity. The girls cheered for strangers at home games.

Colleen's two best friends went to school in Winona. I would come to love Winona, but I don't think it was a welcoming place for the Rollingstone kids. It was one of those insecure midwestern towns that, because it aspired to a suburban smoothness, disdained the farm towns around it. Its high school was a modernist prison, two windowless wings, and the kids who were bussed there would be eight or nine newcomers dispersed into a class of five hundred, into a group of kids who had gone to Winona schools together and played sports together for years.

The difference in the principals illustrated the difference in the schools. Sister Conrad had resigned her position in Rollingstone over a matter of conscience because she disagreed with the administrators of the diocese and now worked with Catholic Services—with unwed mothers, with the poor—in Winona. Sister Conrad and the other nuns at Holy Trinity spoke in the vulnerable, questing, sometimes guitar-Mass dopey diction of Vatican II. Separation of church and state aside, Principal Hitt in Winona was by all indications a good man who was competent at a demanding job. But he was also a former jock who became animated only around sports. He would never stand up and announce how he "yearns to explain" how he "conceives of [the school] in the world of today." He would never invoke his "respect and love for the entire human family" and find that anything in him demanded "engaging . . . in a conversation." His heroes did not enter "this world to give witness to the truth, to rescue and not sit in judgment, to serve and not to be served." Wally Hitt would rather die than talk like that. The language of this new place was the language of the pep rally, the language of obedience and enthusiasm.

The promise of Vatican II—the promise of conversation about the deepest things—would not be fulfilled. For good constitutional reasons, public schools are hobbled when they address the questions of the spirit that are the life of the soul: Why am I here? What is the good life? Is there a greater purpose? The concept of love could be discussed in Holy Trinity School. And, because Principal Hitt stashed coaches in the social studies departments, even the *Room 222*-style discussions about contemporary society didn't happen much (which is probably no great loss). At Holy Trinity, where one out of ten students entered the clergy, the highest good was sainthood. At Winona High, it was winning the big game. The problem with jock culture is not that it exalts sports—sports are great—but that it scorns everything else.

One of the boys who'd had to finish high school in Winona said that he and his friends spent those high school years stoned. But his wasn't the celebratory *Man, the sixties were something* tone usually adopted when invoking that period. Twenty-five years later, he said that he had never been more depressed. Colleen's friends talked about the anger that would surprise them in those years. While a few viewed the new school as energizing, the language of most of Colleen's friends was the bruised, baffled language of children who'd been through a divorce. It was the language of children whose most intimate culture had been destroyed.

THE FIRST CITY I KNEW WELL was TV's Gotham, the site of Batman. *It was filled with razory obsidian cars, police commissioners so grim-faced they seemed in the process of becoming their own statues, warehouses that served as tilted palaces for criminals (including the leather-clad Catwoman), society galas glamorous as chandeliers, punches that prompted actual cartoon starbursts, and harassed apartment dwellers who would have tête-à-têtes with Batman and Robin as they rappelled a building face.*

PORTRAIT OF THE ARTIST AS SWINGING BACHELOR SPORTSWRITER

SPORTS DIDN'T JUST GIVE ME FRIENDSHIPS. THEY GAVE me cities. The North Stars played in the old Met Center, where the Mall of America now stands in Bloomington, which borders Minneapolis. I talked the family into attending a North Stars game.*

We encountered freeways for the first time. Freeways were like higher math problems. There were some people who could navigate them, but not us and not anyone we knew. There were too many possibilities, too many decisions, too little forgiveness. One had to know one's exit, plan one's lane changes, and negotiate with other drivers. Decisions were coefficient, multivariate, interdependent, time sensitive, and proliferating. The imperatives of exits and frontage roads and lanes that spliced and split, that blocked your vision and urged you to accelerate, seemed impossibly unforgiving to us.

---

*In retrospect, I have no idea how we afforded this. It may have been that, while we could never afford the big things we needed, such as tractors and cars and tuition, or make much of a dent in Dad's medical expenses, we could afford this brightness. My sisters may have kicked in. It also confirmed my strange *special* status in the family.

My father got so lost, we thought we were in Canada. Even more than the rest of us, he felt the precariousness of thousands of cars moving at speeds that, if anything went wrong, would kill the occupants. But eventually, after being honked at, after some start-and-stop lurches into lanes, after missed exits and bad directions, we got where we were headed.

Inside the Met Center, which held a crowd the size of twenty Rollingstones, the North Stars moved onto the ice like deft vehicles accelerating into traffic. Sitting among these excited fans, safe behind the Plexiglas boards, we would have been content to simply watch them warm up. But when the game against the Montreal Canadiens—probably the best hockey team on the planet that year—began, they moved even faster, harassing each other with their sticks, sending passes across the ice, and crunching each other into the boards. The boards continued to vibrate after the play had moved on. Shots pinged the glass. At one point, a North Star swooped behind the net and just as he turned to head up ice, a Canadien intersected him with such force that the Plexiglas panel beneath us evaporated.

From its freeways to its sports, the Twin Cities had felt like a crash about to happen, and now it had happened: the panel had popped loose, hitting a girl who later received stitches. We knew we were supposed to feel sympathy for whoever was hit by the detached Plexiglas, but we felt a strange mix of relief and glamour. The game went on, and our gratefulness at having a story to tell made us love it even more. We couldn't stop talking about the speed and beauty of the game. We were Catholics; we expected miracles, and there was something brutally angelic in what we had seen. Professional hockey was to the sports we knew—kickball in the yard, basketball in the high school gym—as the Batmobile was to our John Deere tractor.

We stayed at the Thunderbird Motel, which was within walking distance of the Met Center. It struck me as quite swank, with its vivid totem pole sign and its daring red carpets and ice machines and color televisions.

Strange as it seems, this motel on a suburban frontage road reawakened for me an image of cities as glamorous places. It animated the images inspired by Petula Clark's "Downtown." I thought that it would be terribly cool to live in the Thunderbird Motel and be a sportswriter.

I viewed myself as a bachelor in my fantasy life as a grown-up sportswriter because at least this eight-year-old boy lived in a world where, except for the baffling visitations of crushes, girls were simply irrelevant. Being a bachelor seemed fun. I was a year or two away from understanding sex; it was still a baffling urgency in the groin and a wavery feeling in the stomach. Sex in the sixties seemed like an endless Twister game with Goldie Hawn and Julie Newmar.

Christmas break 1967. I flipped on the TV, which broadcast a football game—the NFL championship between the Green Bay Packers and the Dallas Cowboys.

The temperature was seventeen below zero. Players' breath crystallized in front of them. Breathing suddenly seemed masculine and monstrous. Players shivered on the sidelines. A full game was played, but for me, it evaporated like the players' breath, resolving itself into a single highlight: time running out, the Packers at the goal line, the great human sledges of the lines facing each other, Bart Starr behind center taking the snap. Suddenly Jerry Kramer threw a block that slid Cowboy defensive tackle Jethro Pugh to the right. Starr slid into the vacated sliver of space and across the goal line. In its deft leverage and cascading efficiency, Kramer's block was artistic. More specifically, when I contemplated what happened—an arrangement altered just enough, Jethro Pugh nudged—what remained in the mind was as beautiful as a perfectly kerned sentence. Of course, in the line, bones were crunched, skin abraded, flesh bruised, brains jostled. Men swore and grabbed and grunted. Only a mind absolutely famished for design would see the satisfactions of typography in men smashing each other with the force of machines.

I started to write. In August of 1968, when I was nine, I was undergoing my annual semiquarantine from hay fever. Late every summer, I would sneeze through a box or two of Kleenex a day, my head would fill up, my eyes would water and itch, and I would have to stay inside (even though we couldn't afford an air conditioner) and take Contac or Allerest, both of which made me sleep half the day and sit on the couch in a bleary trance the other half.

I began to write recaps of every Minnesota Vikings game on ruled, three-hole-punched paper. Even though I love sports, my mind sometimes wanders during games. The need to later summarize the game focused me, and I wonder, as I note this, if writing for me is not a therapeutic note-taking, less an outlet than an inlet—it forces me to notice the world. I collected my recaps in something I called my Vikings Book. My handwriting twitched over the thin blue rules. I composed breathless accounts of Bill Brown "smashing ahead to victory" and Fred Cox "putting it out of reach" with a late field goal and the "Vikes giving it their best" in a "losing effort." I clipped photographs of the team from the *Winona Daily News.* The players were shockingly young, the paper disturbingly antique—peach-colored, brittle. I drew little pictures of elongated, lumpy players. I gave awards for best offensive, defensive, and overall players for the game. I took chances with headlines. I actually wrote, "Vikes Snip Redskins." (I think I meant "Nip.")

When I think of what the Vikings meant to me, the words *role model,* which are so often invoked in public discussions of athletes, seem to miss the point. I experienced pro athletes as comic book heroes miraculously made human, as beings who did something more intense, more clashing, more precise, more graceful, more resonant than anything in daily life. I think I suspected then that professional athletes are in a tricky netherworld between art and life. On the one hand, because they concentrate their efforts into an intense final product, a costumed performance, a sixty-minute game, their private lives are irrelevant. But they are both the actor and the character. When an actor steps off stage, he is no longer Hamlet. When Vikings running back Bill Brown stepped off the field, he was still Bill Brown. And athletes were artists we rooted for, and to root for something, you have to persuade yourself that it's morally superior. Fortunately, everyone more or less behaved themselves, and in December, when opposing teams shivered by space heaters in Metropolitan Stadium, the Vikings stood at attention, the snow falling on their bare heads with no heaters in sight, like the warriors they were.

I loved my Vikings Book, but I didn't quite like it. On the front of the blue three-ring binder, I'd adhered a sticker, a cartoon drawing of a man scratching his stomach with the title "Fat Slob." I hated the way my hand and eyes never quite drew a graceful line or letterform. I hated my ugly drawings. I hated the way I couldn't even judge the simplest line breaks. One of my headlines read:

Vikings Kill Cowboy
s

Ultimately, my hands betrayed my attempts at writing just as my larynx and tongue and teeth betrayed my attempts at speaking. I wanted to escape the sloppiness of the self. I wanted the beautifully regular patterns I could make with a Spirograph. I wanted what typographers, designers, photographers, illustrators, and printers could provide, although I had no idea people made their living as typographers and designers. The urge to write is obviously noble; I understood that I was honoring the Vikings. And I knew from *Wonders of the Animal Kingdom* that writing was a superior form of collecting because, unlike, say, a bunch of butterflies pinned to a surface, *stories* about butterflies both preserved *and animated* them. But writing also shares something with addiction. Like the addict, the writer is not quite comfortable with the awkward present and the ugly self.

There was nothing necessary about my Vikings Book—the newspapers covered the games. I had no special audience, no new material, no distinctive style. I was ten. Nobody cared what I wrote. But when I composed those accounts, something resolved itself in me.

PEANUTS *WALLPAPERED MY childhood. Linus's vigil for the Great Pumpkin was* Waiting for Godot *for eight-year-olds. Their morals, which I still find embarrassingly inspiring, fused with my memories of Christmas and Halloween.*

Peanuts *was the opposite of sports. My love of sports was a love of excellence, of movement, of competence that sweetened into heroism. In the most famous frame in* Peanuts, *Lucy pulls the football away. Charlie Brown thuds on his ass.* Peanuts *inventories the dull sabotage of the self. I didn't precisely like Charles Schulz's creation, but it resonated with me. I now know why. Except for Snoopy, all the characters are nominally children but essentially middle-aged—floating in a miasma of low self-esteem (Pigpen), clinging to their addictions (Linus), controlling the world through sheer bossiness (Lucy). And then there is Charlie Brown—bald, burdened, depressed, anxious, self-doubting, clad in a dull shirt. The emotions of my childhood were often not what we think of as childlike—that is, they were often not insouciant. The emotional life of children is as neurotic as that of adults, maybe more so because children have less insight, less perspective, and less control.*

BASEBALL CARDS AND THE PROBLEM OF EVIL

SPORTS WERE A BOYHOOD FANTASY THAT SHOWED glimpses of the real pressures of adult life. When I looked at baseball cards, I didn't fully see the darknesses behind the pleasing designs and heroic poses. Let's say, grabbing five cards from a collection I reassembled in the 1990s—for much more money than I spent in 1967—that I held numbers 8, 9, 39, 48, and 56 in the Topps 1967 series: the beak-nosed, frowning Ron Hansen; the thick-browed, sluggish-faced Chuck Harrison; the doe-faced, sad-eyed José Tartabull; Bill Freehan, poised, catcher's mitt forward, hand cocked to throw, squinting and dissolved into the game; Curt Simmons, mouth tightened into a smile or scowl, capless, crew cut, with hatchety features. At the time, did I see the anxiety on every face but Freehan's? I flipped the cards over, and statistics suggested stories. Hansen had only batted seventy-four times the year before. Harrison had been in the majors only one tenuous year. Tartabull had been traded halfway through the last season. One of the little cartoons on his card said, "José was originally the property of the San Francisco Giants." Simmons's card notes only that he led the National League in shutouts in 1952—fifteen years earlier. For tax purposes, baseball players are property; they can be depreciated, like equipment. Baseball cards are photographed in spring training, when men's jobs are at risk.

One football season, Pete Maus lent me *Instant Replay,* Jerry Kramer's account of his year with the Packers. It was the first book I ever read, and it was by an offensive lineman, the most unlikely of authors.

In football, running backs' improvisations could be described as poetry in motion. Slow down tape of receivers enough and you can see the ballet in their sprints and leaps. Quarterbacks had some of the tactical intelligence of military commanders, and even defensive players had a barbarian charm (like barbarians, they sacked things). But offensive linemen were the sons of mill workers and miners and farmers; they were subterranean and flinching men, lunks even by football standards, charged with fortifying the quarterback and bulldozing defenders out of the way of running backs.

Kramer writes of one game, "I got the hell beat out of me somewhere in the first quarter or the second, I don't know which, I got kicked or something. And I got a slight concussion." He lost his memory of plays less than two years old and notes, "I don't have any idea how long I played today. I don't have any idea and I won't until I see the movies." He got up the next morning and went deer hunting.

On the book's cover, Kramer looks gladiatorial. He rests on a bench, hands dangling between his knees. He's so muddy, he might have emerged from a mine. He stares at the ground as if exhausted from combat. He resembles my father if my father had been healthy: broad shoulders (accentuated with pads), thickened forearms, regular features—brisker than my father's—and a thatch of brown hair. And, like my father, he was raised on a farm—or a ranch that sounded a lot like a farm.

And he resembled my father in a deeper way. Both men lived with great pain and the threat of losing everything they had worked for. Kramer talks of players forced to play with shoulder separations. The defensive lineman Henry Jordan quit because he decided "that the rewards of football just weren't worth the pain anymore." Kramer calls Red Mack "the flanker we picked up last season after he was cut by the team with the worst record in the league . . . I'll never forget the look on his face after we won the Super Bowl, walking around the locker room in his jockstrap, hugging everybody, tears just running down his face, and he was saying, 'This is the greatest moment of my life.'" Mack was cut from the squad; he "just packed up and left without saying good-bye. I don't think he wanted to face anybody."

As an adult, I felt pride when I learned that Kramer had written *Instant Replay* because the editor Dick Schaap had stopped in to see Kramer's roommate only to find Kramer, alone, reading Wallace Stevens aloud. Was I proud to learn that farm boys were not all rubes?

Or was I proud that Kramer was not, *really,* a farmer but an *author?* My father took roostery pleasure in the fact that, when he went into Winona dressed in a shirt and tie, people would mistake him for "an executive." He went through a dozen surgeries to farm again, but he did not want to be seen as a farmer.

* * *

Throughout high school, Dennis kept getting hurt. He sprinted up a hay elevator—a conveyor that forms a hypotenuse between the hay wagon and the loft—tripped, fell, and broke his arm. We knew what that drop was like because we would throw hay bales down from the second story; the impact broke the bales open.

Or, with his shirttail out, as was the fashion at the time, Dennis leaned against the stove. A burner ignited his shirttail, so he raced around the kitchen table and leapt into the sink, which was brimming with sudsy water.

Twice during basketball games, Dennis drove for a layup and an opposing player ran under him, spinning Dennis like a pinwheel, and his head hit the parquet floor. Both times, he was taken to the hospital for observation but released. From running the farm to serving as class president, Dennis was the essence of responsible. But something wild and unresolved seemed to flare inside him, too.

From the time he was five, Dennis worked with Dad in the fields, accompanied him everywhere, and, as he got older, ran the farm himself. "Older" here is perhaps misleading. At the end of his freshman year, when he was fourteen, he went into the principal's office and asked if he could be flunked. When Sister Conrad asked him why he would request such a thing—his grades were fine—he replied that he was so busy running the farm that he didn't want to have to worry about school. He thought of this solution himself and asked Sister Conrad not to tell Mom and Dad. She didn't, but she also didn't flunk him. Given this history, he could reasonably expect that his years of service would be paid off. The Herber boys would inherit their father's farms or have the wherewithal to buy nearby farms. Down the road, Pete Faber would inherit the farm from Ray. Steve Speltz inherited the farm from Frank. But Dennis wouldn't inherit our farm; the debt was simply too heavy.

After graduating from high school, where he was the star basketball player and the president of his small senior class, Dennis attended Winona State. But he inserted obscenities into his papers, as if trying to pick a fight. He read Camus and yearned to commit violent, absurd acts. He worked at a nearby farm and, I found out years later, drank by himself every night. Then he quit drinking.

And then he did something no one expected. He enlisted in the Marines during the middle of the Vietnam War.

* * *

In fourth grade, Sister Maureen let John Kendrick and me ask questions about ultimate matters of heart and soul and existence, as well as the stump-the-Deity questions that Catholicism seems to breed. (A George Carlin routine: "Say, Faddah, if God is all powerful, can he make a rock so big that he himself can't lift it?")

We asked improbable hypotheticals: *If you and another child are starving and you secretly discover a candy bar, should you share it?* Yes, says Sister Maureen, the Gospel counsels love, and love means sharing what we have. *Even if there is only enough for one?* Perhaps here Sister fumbles, but she recovers. Yes, remember the loaves and the fishes. God will provide. Sister Maureen kept repeating that "God is love" and, since religion was the study of God, religion was the study of love. She would repeat, "Wherever two or more of you are gathered in my name, there I shall be," and this recipe for a deity never left me even though it would be decades before I understood what she meant.

I did not precisely have a crush on Sister Maureen. I knew what a crush felt like because I'd had one on Kathy Meyers, and I knew the sense of pleasant obsession, the recurrence of her image in my mind, my nervousness when she was around, and this wasn't that. But there was something in my relation to Sister Maureen that would not have been there with a male teacher. The "something" is hard to define—a solicitude, a softness, a wanting to please, an opening up, whatever it is in the tone of any private letter that causes a blush if it is accidentally made public.

Did John and I pose the problem of evil to Sister Maureen? I can't remember. But the question—*if an all-good, all-powerful being exists, why does he tolerate such awfulness?*—percolated through my life. Bad things happened. Our dog, Fluffy—with her thin nose, lustrous black hair, and intelligent brown eyes—had been missing for some weeks. One purple-silver dusk, while I was walking in the weedy ditch along the road between our farm and the Herbers', I stumbled upon Fluffy's corpse. She was fly-bothered, maggot-pimpled, stiff, and light as cardboard. She stank. She'd been shot with a shotgun, so her guts were exposed.

In a few years, I would stumble upon the freshly shot corpse of a man killed in a drug deal, and the feeling was the same: a patina of motive, a nimbus of evil, hovered above the murdered body. When I looked at Fluffy, her eyes were full of shocked vacancy, and her black hair, as pretty as eyelashes, was matted with blood.

I put her in a burlap bag and brought her to the backyard and held a funeral for her. I wore my dad's purple bathrobe to simulate priest's vestments and gathered whoever was willing to humor me—Colleen, Karl Herber—and said some prayers over Fluffy and sprinkled her with water that I had declared holy and then buried her.

I don't think I posed the problem about evil to Sister Maureen. For all their inquisitiveness, my questions had an emotionally blank, academic quality. Religion became culture in me, but it did not become faith.

Why did belief fail to take when I was so immersed and so innocent, when those around me really did live their faith? It's possible that, in attempting to undo the shaming excesses of fifties Catholicism, sixties Catholicism erred in the opposite direction, toward a folksinger God. "God is love" sounds like a simple formulation, but it is in fact a problematic one. If God is love, then God is not everything because there is much that has nothing whatsoever to do with love. And if God is not everything, then God is small. The emphasis on a loving God meant a de-emphasis on the arbitrary, punishing God of the Old Testament. I do not believe we read Job, where a just man loses everything to a whimsical God, or Ecclesiastes, which tells us that life is unfair and that the race is not always to the swift. "God is love" can devolve into "God is nice."

Whatever force detonated the car that carried my father when he was eighteen and detached his nose and lips and scrambled his life was not nice. Whatever universal power pulsed through the brains and hands of the doctors who worked on my father but could not fix him was not nice. I was taught Mark and Luke at school, but it was the Old Testament God who shaped my father's life. Jesus didn't shatter hips and scrape off noses and lips. And as a result, I was never angry with God as a child. I never prayed, except as reflexive desperation. The God of religion class somehow didn't matter—didn't touch the moment, didn't live in the room.

But blaming my religion teachers seems fatuous. When it comes to shaping children, religion is, so to speak, damned if it does and damned if it doesn't. A catechism that acknowledged pain wouldn't have helped, either. Belief never coagulated in my blood because pain never entered my heart.

Spiritually, I had a lot of growing up to do. In high school, anger would be the first step toward belief—you can't hate the nonexistent—and, as an adult, alcohol—soothing, connecting, resonance-making—would serve as a strange prototype of faith. And drinking would lead me to faith in another way. After alcohol would dominate me, when I would wake in a bed soupy with vomit, when my brain throbbed like a heart, when I scrambled to remember what I had done and dreaded what I had to do to make things at least sort of right, I finally felt my incompleteness, the sense of self as shard. I stepped toward faith. It was only after all this that faith as I know it now—the sense of personal transformation and refuge, the sense of God as a kind of secret oxygen, the sense of alignment with the sweetest possibilities of the universe—would become real for me. But as a kid in Rollingstone, I was decades away from that. I experienced hurt without quite feeling pain, which is itself dangerous.

IT SEEMED LIKE CAR CRASHES were everywhere in the sixties. Two of my teenage cousins died in a crash in Illinois. Mangled cars and teenage corpses appeared in newspapers and cautionary TV specials.

Milo, the oldest of Ralph Herber's children, missed a turn less than a mile from our house late one night while returning from a dance in Lewiston. When Ralph stopped by a family reunion decades later, I noticed in his wallet, which was teeming with images of grandchildren, a photo from the sixties—Beatles haircut, Buddy Holly glasses—and realized it was Milo's high school picture.

UNSUSTAINABLE FARMING

MY PARENTS WOULD TELL STORIES ABOUT THEIR CHILDhood Christmases in the Depression: how one year, my father got a pencil. Or how another year, my mother received an orange. We thought that these were standard cautionary tales about gratefulness. But I think these stories were a way of preparing us for the poverty that trembled on the horizon.

How poor were we? I now know that one year in the late sixties, at the time that I was hauling in my load of Christmas loot, our family income was $8,000 and our medical bills were $300,000. And there was something else I didn't notice: during the 1967–68 school year, my parents had five children and a farm ten miles from where Mom worked, and they did not own a car. My brother had a used Pontiac that served as the family car. Our previous car burned so much oil that, when we idled at stop signs, we pretended to smoke cigarettes to explain the cloud billowing around us. Dennis and Maureen and Mom would drive into town every morning when Mom went into work, or else they would figure out a way to get back to pick up Mom for a three-to-eleven shift.

Dad wasn't getting better. After one of his surgeries, he returned in a cast that mummified his legs and torso, immobilizing his legs, atrophying his muscles, festering unreachably taunting itches. He lived with the cast for some days, but at some point, he couldn't stand it. He and Mom yelled at each other. He grabbed his crutches. Because he used them to move his whole body, his arms were as strong as legs. He swung himself in angry, pendulous increments out of the house. Mom stayed on the couch and wept. He went into the shed—negotiating the stone steps, grabbing a saw without falling over—and in a fit of rage fed by too many years of not being the man he wanted to be, of not being the man implied in the basketball player who got into that car in 1938, he ignored the instructions of his doctor and the tears of my mother and sawed off his cast.

I don't think I went a day without thinking about the car crash that forever changed my father's life—its screech and shatter, its blood and weeping and shock, pulsed with an almost religious power. It sounds silly to say that Dad's crash felt like a creation myth, but it sounds dishonest not to say that. Without the crash, Dad never would have met Mom. But he would have lived a very different life.

I can't feel what my father felt, but it is one of the imperatives of memoir not simply to tell our own stories but to inhabit adjacent stories. I got the slightest glimpse of my father's life in my early thirties when I was single and feverish with a bladder infection, and I had to spend a couple of days home from work. I spent the time in my apartment alone, marinating in my fever, my thoughts petty and grandiose and strange, with only the degraded companionship of the TV. Sleep and waking melted into a single, unsatisfying continuum. I lay unshowered, half-dressed, unventilated. I kicked at covers ropy and uncomfortable and adversarial.

And I got another glimpse of Dad's private world when I was about eight and I went sledding over at Karl Herber's. On the other side of the Herbers' yard, the land sloped down into the valley. We sledded on this incline on beautiful wooden sleds with red metal runners. Sliding head first, stomach down, I lifted my face to see in front of me. I pushed off. Snow vibrated at my chin. The incline where we would tumble and abandon our sleds approached.

About halfway down, my sled veered right, discovered snow coated with ice, and accelerated toward a collection of discarded garbage cans, rusty and filled with burnt garbage. That slimy can targeted me like gravity. Time changed in a way that is called slow motion but isn't quite: the moment syruped in my mind and panicked in my body. The garbage can loomed, sight dissolved into impact, and I was sprawling, stopped; I lay on the snow as traumatized as a newborn; my sled was somewhere else. I got up and staggered. The Herbers, whose sleds had slid safely down the other ravine, appeared and guided me toward the house. I sensed a sliding on my face and saw red on the snow. I was bleeding. I sensed a second slipperiness on my face gliding over the first. My head shook. I was crying. The Herbers' pretty teenage sister, Jeannie, ran down from the house. The Herbers got me cleaned up and home.

I spent that pearly overcast February afternoon at home on the couch, watching sports on our black and white TV. I kept touching my cut face as if it were Braille and it would tell me something; I accepted offerings of Nestle's Quik and ice cream, which I mixed with my spoon into a sweet sludge. I feared the impending trip to the doctor for a shot, and I let the television images swarm in the place where my thoughts should be. I knew the planet could be a bully. I knew the taunts of physics. I knew a little of what my father knew. But just a little. A sled is not a car. A couch is not a hospital bed. A cut face isn't a crushed hip. A day ending in ice cream is not a decade ending in failure.

What surprises me looking back isn't the despair my parents felt but how bravely they fought against it. One Christmas, we decorated the spruce tree outside the house with blue lights. As

Mom and Dad backed up the car onto the road on their way to a New Year's Eve party, they were so transfixed by the blue lights against the green branches in the middle of our snowy farmstead that—sober, laughing like champagne—they backed into the ditch. The moral: *Dad is sick. The family is broke. But that does not mean that we cannot feel joy.*

Around fourth grade, some fears crystallized into facts: Dad wasn't getting better, and the medical bills kept mounting. Dennis's entry into the Marines confirmed that the farm was moribund. The farm was sold to the Herbers, and we were told of a new house about five miles away on a road by Minnesota City, the village between us and Winona.

An auction was held. People stood in our driveway. Our things became merchandise. We milled in our driveway like spectators. The auctioneer sold our machinery: the skinny tractor with the perforated, pelvis-shaped seat; the suddenly antique milk cans; the buckets that held feed and water; the special pails with the nipples at the bottom that fed calves; all of it. The Herbers needed our land, not our outdated equipment.

The auctioneer fascinated me because he had some of the charisma of sportscasters. He used his voice to fascinate and create. His voice seemed unreal, as if he had been born with a harmonica in his throat.

The blankness of my memories of this time troubles me. A few details are vivid, the chronology is apparent, and grey skies pervade my recollections, although they should not be taken as a simple analog for sadness. I've associated overcast skies with dismalness, but I've also welcomed them for the way they've made working inside seem more inviting and playing outside feel more crisp, for the way their moodiness can stand in for some of the sublimity of the sea. I consider too much good weather banal. But I fear that those overcast skies of that last fall on the farm might have been placeholders for other feelings.

I don't remember talking with my parents about moving. I

don't remember discussions about school (arrangements were made for me to continue to attend Holy Trinity). I don't remember packing. I don't remember making any cinematic final survey of the place, walking the yard from the apple orchard in the east lawn to the evergreen copse that served as a windbreak on the western side of the house, visiting the vacated, scrubbed barn and the corn shed with stray shucks scritching across the floor, hiking the pasture and my odd shrines of birch trees, lichen-covered rocks, and raspberry brambles. I don't remember taking any leave of the Herber boys. I don't remember helping carry boxes to the car. I don't remember anyone else's reaction.

Our house emptied, and its hidden ugliness suddenly surfaced: the tile, yellow as chicken fat, under the refrigerator; the dust prairies under beds; and then, the indifference of a place you have vacated.

As we drove away, I sat in the backseat and turned. Our house diminished in my sight. The orchard moved past. When I later studied art history, I would think of the expressionism of its trees (gnarled, overcast-colored, human-sized) and the impressionism of its blossoms.

The Herbers' place passed behind my back, out of my vision, but then again, the fields I looked at were now theirs, too. We owned nothing here. Then, as we descended the hill, the pearled sky and the stubble of harvested fields and the crown of the homestead disappeared. I began to look forward as well as backward, left as well as right, jutting my head like a dog startled by the fragrant world as a thickness of trees thinned to reveal the Speltzes' cow pond below; as we turned onto the valley road that pointed toward Rollingstone and passed the Lehnertzes' cows, unambitious as landscape, baffled by our movement; as we entered Rollingstone, thick with the houses of classmates; as we passed the park where the yellow forks had surged across the green grass and we had scattered after them; as we passed the oak-dignified cemetery; and as we passed the gym that Dennis had made incandescent with his basketball playing, as if the energy of his playing illuminated its lights and amplified its crowd. As we proceeded forward, we erased the landscape.

We passed the chocolate-brick school. I would still attend even after it became a public school in fifth grade. This arrangement clearly took some effort on my parents' part (my dad's part, I've since learned). There would be that one connection yet, and so the rest of what I would view on this trip would, in some altered way, still be a part of my life. The rest of the family would spend their days in other places. We passed the convent with its hidden female life, and Arnoldy's Store with its festival of candies and bubblegum cards. On my left, the street where we lived for one year when I was three—and where I had later accompanied Dad to the creamery and where I had been an honorary Kreidemacher brother—telescoped into a glimpse and disappeared as we passed Klinger's Bar with its sunlightlike beer and beerlike sunlight. And then we drove out of town, fields appearing again, past the Kendricks', past the stream where we had imagined Dakota warriors, and then past the Literskis'. As the road continued, the landscape wasn't unknown—this was where we drove to get groceries; this was where Mom went to work—but it was unfamiliar. Its sights didn't touch my mind like words.

Minnesota City was less a town than a series of roads dispersed along the Mississippi River like shed snake skins. Our new place, a farmhouse from which the farm had long been amputated, was on one of those roads. We turned onto it just before we reached Highway 61; it ran north for about a half mile, paralleling the highway and the river. We were the first house on the right, just after a strange, stray hayfield, a remnant of the time when this had been farmland. Our big, century-old house stood amid new, modest construction. There were oak trees and maples in our yard and a barn, which we would use as a garage.

Below our house, down a wooded incline, a backwater gathered, orphaned from the river that flowed past on the other side of Highway 61, dotted with muskrat mounds. It looked too stewy to hold fish.

The house was sadder than our house in Rollingstone. It was an old people's house; its previous owners had moved into a retirement home. There was no furnace; a vast space heater squatted in the kitchen. We would wake up cold that winter and hurry to the kitchen, but we would wake at different times and go different places. I ascended the stairs to my room, which was tucked in a corner, too far away from the girls' room to yell knock-knock jokes, too far away from the space heater to be heated well. I discovered dead flies in my windowsills. They were light and abundant, a popcorn of corpses.

I started to put up my sports decorations. Oddly, the first things I put up were old covers of *Sport* from the fifties. The colors of the fifties were different, slightly washed out.

II MINNESOTA CITY

FLIRTING WITH NUNS

I COULD NOT BEAR TO BREAK UP WITH ROLLINGSTONE. So every school-day morning, I walked down our spur of road to Highway 248, and I waited for Miss Gappa. Riding to school with a teacher couldn't have been more different from riding to school, smushed and squealing in the pickup, with my brother and sisters. Miss Gappa was Holy Trinity's only lay teacher. She commuted from Winona, and it was kind of her to pick me up. It stuck a ten-year-old, spastic with conversation, into the quiet part of her day.

Holy Trinity Elementary was in its last year. The nuns would be leaving, the crucifixes taken down, the cut-paper apostles removed, and the holy water fonts drained. The holy water fonts made me realize what the grade school me hated about Protestants—their cultural dehydration. They had no staring icons, no sonorous liturgy, no purple robes, no bruised saints, no graceful nuns, no silver-skied holy cards, no sponges resting in pools of water, no prospering dilemmas (how is God both all-powerful and all-good?), no administrative code of the soul, no daily Masses (their daily devotion appeared to be business). Of course, I knew no Protestants. They were a bullying blankness.

After school, as I waited for Miss Gappa to finish her work, I wandered in the empty building, which smelled even more fragrantly of Pine-Sol because this was when the custodial staff did their work. I stepped outside to exorcise chalk from erasers. I lingered by the guardrail and the birch-lined slope on the road south of the school. But I spent most of my time with the nuns, especially Sister Maureen.

I shared with the nuns the three handwritten pages of the novel I was writing about three Minnesota North Stars and their swinging bachelor lives. Fortunately for the sisters, my idea of swinging bachelor life was formed by Maxwell Smart on *Get Smart,* and my few pages never got past my heroes' return to their suites at the Thunderbird Motel. I used the word *ironic,* which Sister Patricia noted was advanced for a fourth grader. I wanted to impress these women—with their nyloned legs and heels, with their sky-blue habits and coifs that abstracted the flow of their hair. While I was a few years away from speculating about the nakedness of women, from animating them in my fantasies, the ingredients of longing were there.

And, of all the things I was losing (farm, school, town), Sister Maureen and Sister Patricia were the part of that fading world to which I could say, *Please don't go.* Or I could almost say such things. I could hang around and make a nuisance of myself. I could write three pages of an awful novel. If I'd been a more athletic boy, I would have simply stood on my head and waited for them to tell me I was special.

I poked around the new place in Minnesota City. In the disused barn, I found wooden orange crates with circuslike graphics, grease guns sweating iridescent pastes, and stencil-printed wooden drawers that held rusted nails and screws. An outhouse stank in one corner of the garage. I stared into the shitty abyss.

I missed the reassurances of design. The cow manure and pig squealing can obscure the fact that farms are designs: literal fields of color, icons of white houses and red barns and green tractors, the hefty rectangular bales of hay, even the spacing and serifs of cornstalks. And like designs, farms had a purpose: they were arranged to get things done. Compared to this, Minnesota City just seemed slovenly—an unused field here, a ravine there, a gouged sand quarry, a swamp. Our barn was a spooky vestige.

I overlooked much—the great elegant river on the other side of the highway, the beautiful bluffs just beyond the houses. And, closer to home, the barn could become a clubhouse. The swamp below our house, a rink. The front yard, a baseball diamond. But that would require friends.

On the weekends, I played alone but expectantly, hoping to make those new friends by being in the right place at the right time. At age ten, I could still spend hours outside, moving with the darting secret logic of a dog, and no one would care. I walked the perimeter of our yard and wandered up and down the road. I mimed games of football. I'd never learned to ride a bike—it was pointless on the farm—so I didn't range much beyond our driveway. I missed the Herbers.

On one of those snowless November Saturdays, I loitered in the yard, hoping to make friends, and a black-haired crane of a kid approached on his bike. He pedaled fast, then *stood on the bike seat* and rode it like a surfboard, and as it veered into a ditch and toppled, he leapt off. Thus, I met Greg Bingold, my first Minnesota City friend. I introduced myself. The best course of action seemed to be to get together and play Hot Wheels.

The holidays intervened, but then, one weekend afternoon in January, bundled faces appeared at the door: Greg Bingold flanked by two boys named Jeff Brust and Gary Mahaffey and, behind them, smaller children and adults reassuring as trees. Smiling, their heads wrapped in parka hoods, with the balloon faces of children in cartoons, the three boys announced they were going sledding in the quarry by our house. For some reason I can't now recover—maybe shyness, maybe some other plans—

I did not go with them. But a life as a boy—a life of games, a life of buddies—seemed possible here.

* * *

By spring, we were playing a version of baseball—the ball itself was soft, the positions improvised, the bases exposed roots and Frisbees. We played the way boys used to play, before all sports became organized sports: without supervision, with no one watching, negotiating our own disagreements. If the Frisbee that was second base were, say, accidentally kicked into the outfield, this raised the question of whether the Frisbee was the base or simply marked the base, and that sometimes raised the question of Jeff Brust's precise state of mind when he kicked it, and conflict led to conflict resolution, which took the form of maxims such as "tie goes to the runner" and which further took the form of tackling each other and wrestling until someone agreed that a given interpretation of events was the most reasonable. We achieved consensus by asphyxiation. We wanted a pitcher, not a belly itcher.

* * *

At the end of the school year, the nuns left Holy Trinity. I wrote them letters. The graceful loops and modest descenders in their responses reminded me of the habits they wore.

I DETERMINED TO LEARN HOW to ride a bike. Jeff Brust lent me his old Schwinn, gave me some advice, and spotted me as best he could. I would start, wobble, and fall; start, wobble, and fall; start, coast a few feet, wobble, and, because I'd picked up more speed, fall harder. At some point, my steps churned a stream of motion that gravity couldn't tug back to earth. I counted twenty-two bruises that first night, but the next day, as I stepped on the pedals and animated the bike, I wondered what had been so difficult. I could get to Jeff's or Gary's house quickly, and along the way, I could enjoy the private breeze and blur of riding. I looked forward to the lightness in the gut when I let the bike pick up momentum down an incline, and I savored the machine-multiplied power of my legs when I pumped up that same incline on the way home.

WHAT IS A VILLAGE?

I RODE MY BIKE DOWN HIGHWAY 248 AND SOUTH ON Highway 61, past the sand quarries and the L-Cove Bar, for a mile or so until I reached my new town. It is hard to imagine that two villages three miles apart could be so different.

Once in Minnesota City, I pumped up the hill to the church and school and ball field, and then I accelerated giddily down again, turning right on Minnesota City's one apparent street to the post office and a swinging foot bridge. Another street threaded back to the first. Then, tottering over railroad tracks, I followed a road that looped away from the town and toward the river and back again. And that was Minnesota City, although half the people whose kids went to the school lived elsewhere, along yet another road in the scraggly land between the highway and the river, on a development tucked into the bluffs by the highway.

Wilfrid Sheed wrote of Los Angeles that it seems dangerous to have so many people and not have a city. Pedaling in search of Minnesota City, it seemed wrong to have so few people and not have a village. Villages tug life toward them. In Rollingstone, farmers drove to the creamery, to the feed mill, to the lumberyard, to the bank, to the bars, to the co-op gas station, to the general store, to the dry goods store, to the park, to the chick hatchery. And these comings and goings, this build-up of hellos and errands, these luminous threadings created something. Minnesota City grown-ups worked and shopped in Winona. Minnesota City had only an elementary school with a ball field and a post office. By the time we moved there, the school district had closed the fifth and sixth grade of the elementary school.

It's possible to underestimate how much Rollingstone and Minnesota City had in common. Both towns were places where the love of parents and happiness of childhood were as invisible but potent as oxygen. Our parents did not supervise our play, but they made its joys possible.

But I encountered a type of home nothing like what I encountered in Rollingstone—places that stunk of unwashed dishes and uncleaned laundry and cigarette smoke. It wasn't only a question of mess. As tended as their farmsteads were, people in Rollingstone had too many kids to have immaculate homes. Our yard wasn't going to be featured in any lifestyle sections any time soon; after their dad died, the Literskis also had an occasionally unedited front yard. The Kendricks' was disheveled in a hippie-ish way, like a harassed co-op. But there was a generosity to such mess. I liked spending time at the Literskis' and Kendricks'. But what I saw here was squalor, mess soaked with tragedy, dangerous boyfriends—stubble-chinned, tank-top-wearing brutes with the power of men and the volatility of children; they frightened us; they plastered their cars with bumper stickers that said, "Candy is Dandy but sex doesn't rot your teeth"; they shared porn with the kids. Such magazines existed on the illicit edge of our consciousness; they certainly weren't anything a trusted adult—which was every Rollingstone adult—would share with you.

The mess I glimpsed here was a nakedness. I wanted to look away. I wanted to leave.

This is, I think, what those old Rollingstone Catholics who railed against "paganism" were afraid of; this is what prompted them to insist on policing every spiritual misdemeanor. The least serious of them simply feared people unlike themselves. But the most serious of those fifties Catholics feared a life given over to booze as incendiary as gasoline, to loneliness quenched by a fuck, to weakness ripened into evil. They feared children who had to fight harder than any kid should have to fight to be decent people. Was their fear excessive? Possibly. Was it trivial? No.

* * *

In this dispersed town, we became a dispersed family. Maureen spent summers in friends' apartments. Dennis was deployed in Okinawa. All the girls had after-school jobs. Colleen was dating. Sheila was about to depart for nursing school. It's easy to make too much of this. All families suffer from a cosmic planned obsolescence. Children leave. But the move to Minnesota City sharpened the sense of loss.

It was the sixties. One morning, my parents found Colleen snoring on top of the freezer in our entryway, her mind still caramelized with sleep and the vestiges of drugs. It felt like eons since the five of us innocently danced to the Beatles. The sixties were not a long strange trip. They were a short strange trip.

Shortly after that, we heard that Dennis had been rotated to Vietnam.

* * *

I was the only one returning to Rollingstone, but it wasn't my Rollingstone. I've always loved the beginning of school. But in the days before the elementary school opened as a public school, I was angry at my dispersing family and discarded town. I fantasized vengeance. I would organize my classmates, confront teachers, and pummel administrators. On the morning before I was to leave for school, a newsreel of insurrection—this was

1970—sputtered in my head. Even though the school district was probably not overjoyed to have a rural elementary school to manage, the takeover of Holy Trinity School by District 861 *felt* like an invasion. The administrators seemed as petty as Anglo-Irish landlords. I fizzed with anger.

When I arrived at school, my rage dissipated because my opponent became human, and I learned for the first time that 90 percent of all my anger was fantasy. Specifically, my opponent became Mrs. Losinski, a nice, experienced teacher, who started our American history course with a chapter on explorers, which prompted me to read books about explorers—thin and illustrated, age-appropriate, sheathed with plastic library coverings; books that showed no sign that, from another perspective, this might be called the Age of Invasion; books that presented the explorers as über–Boy Scouts. I began with Columbus's fraught journeys in stumpy late medieval ships and proceeded to read of John Cabot sailing from London across the frigid, boiling North Atlantic; of da Gama hugging Africa and naming its southern tip the Cape of Storms (which the Portuguese king renamed the Cape of Good Hope); of Magellan's ships limping around the world; and of Henry Hudson pushing his crew too far and being marooned by his men in what would become Hudson Bay.

The map reputedly used by Columbus showed a world like a tabletop, from which a ship could drop like a truant green bean. Dragons menaced the margins of this world, like bogeymen fermenting in a child's closet. In my imaginings, Europe always was cloudy, Catholic, and comfortable. The land voyages in America—by de Soto, by Coronado—didn't hold my interest. Guys trudging and arguing sounded too much like our annual car trips to Illinois. I loved the sea voyages—their origins in the cacophonous and concentrated life of Catholic ports, the epic moodiness of the sea, the ships as vulnerable as a family, and the frisson of everything one knew sliding away.

*

Our own voyage from the farm to the place in Minnesota City had cut our financial losses, but Dad was left with nothing to do, even when he was relatively healthy. According to Mom, Dad briefly tried selling vacuums door to door. He worked for a while driving mail from Winona to Rochester, but he couldn't stand the lifting.

The farmer became a gardener. Dad planted marigolds, with petals rough like cats' tongues, and saw-toothed zinnias in the front yard. I have never liked those clenched, domesticated flowers. He enclosed the porch. A man who once milked and managed a dairy herd, he now occupied his time with leather craft kits. I speculate about my dad's inner life after we arrived in Minnesota City. But my speculation rarely becomes insight. Did grief sour into rage or depression? If so, he tactfully kept it from me. Our house was quieter than it was in Rollingstone, but it was always a comfortable place to be. If depression hovered—and how could it not?—Dad's seemingly trivial projects were acts of bravery and decency.

Every Friday night, though, Dad drove to Klinger's Bar to spend time with his friends amid the comfortable smoke and the charming bottles. He always brought me home a bag of Funyuns. He came home softened and fragrant.

For the most part, we lived separate lives in Minnesota City. But we gathered once. Someone had given Dad a tape recorder for Christmas, so everyone but Dennis gathered in my parents' bedroom. It was as if we'd absorbed the staccato energy of *Laugh-In* and *Get Smart* and other shows we'd watched with Dad on the farm. Maureen sang snatches of "The Lion Sleeps Tonight." Colleen remembered how Maureen would sneak up behind male teachers and mumble, "Hey, baby." Sheila re-created the Warholian pleasures of playing "family" with Maureen, of the imagined ride in the unmoving car, of the horrible medicine. We retold knock-knock jokes. We replayed the cartoon version of Dennis's boyhood—the time he chased Maureen with a rake, the time he sprinted up the hay elevator and broke his arm, the time he danced around the kitchen with his shirttail on fire and extinguished himself in the sink. Then, almost forgetting the recorder, we mimed smoking—two fingers touching and leaving the lips, exhaling—and memorialized our old car that burned so much oil that we would all pretend to smoke. Mom reminded us of the apples and Hershey bars on the cross. We remembered clearing the kitchen and dancing to the first Beatles broadcast, the Sunday-night pizza and pop meals, the rides in the pickup where we tried to knock each other off the tailgate. The tape was an act of buoyant nostalgia. What we did not say was that we would never make a tape celebrating our lives in Minnesota City.

* * *

I keep returning to the image of Dad trying to sell vacuums door to door. Simply doing that work was a kind of failure, and he knew it. This was not the 1930s, when stores were far away. This was not the 1950s, when the country was provisioning subdivisions. This was 1970. America had plenty of vacuum cleaners.

A client of mine who works with sales forces maintains that sales is multiple jobs grouped under one name—that selling a commodity like oats is very different from selling computer systems. But I learned this years too late.

I want to punch through the one-way mirror of memoir and say, *Don't let this discourage you. Try agricultural sales. Hell, try car sales. You are a natural.* But no one is a natural at this, at the most arctic of cold calls—at knocking on the doors of strangers and getting them to buy something in which they've expressed no interest. You don't have the sad, savage charm.

I LOVED CAMPING: THE SMELL of stored canvas, the way papery birch bark could be peeled to start fires, the smell of wood smoke lingering in clothes, the way the berries of red sumac could darken and flavor hot water so we could pretend it was tea, the way a hatchet grabbed and split wood. I enjoyed the game "Eat the Dirt," in which guys sit in a circle, stick a twig in the ground, and take turns flipping a bowie knife in the air. If the knife sticks, they drive the twig deeper into the ground; if the knife flops on the ground without sticking, they pull the twig out with their teeth.

RIBBONS AND MEDALS

THE BOY SCOUTS PROMISE OUTDOOR ADVENTURE, BUT my first encounter with Scouting was literary. I inherited Dennis's 1959 *Boy Scout Handbook,* a substantial paperback softened by use. A uniformed Scout illustrated by Norman Rockwell strode across the cover. Like the *Britannica Junior* and *Wonders of the Animal Kingdom,* the *Boy Scout Handbook* was crisp with categories. It outlined knots, virtues, campfires, plants, animals, first-aid techniques, and merit badges. But unlike those other books, it was also brisk with tasks, and those tasks crystallized *ambition* in me for the first time. In Rollingstone, I had been ill-suited to farming, and I was on the wrong side of average at sports. Schoolwork seemed to be about obedience, not achievement. But this was different, and it was somehow tangled up with my passion for collections.

In the *Boy Scout Handbook,* colored sections designated the ranks, starting with magenta for Tenderfoot. If I mastered the sheet bend, the clove hitch, the square knot, the bowline, and the double half hitch, I would be that much closer to being a Tenderfoot. If I explored "a community of nature" and found in it "at least six kinds of wild mammals, birds, reptiles, or fish or evidence of them," I would be closer to being a Second Class Scout. I was interested in meeting these requirements—in learning the typography of knots, in seeing the images of animals—but then I wanted to move beyond them to the next task and the next badge. I loved how every achievement precipitated an ornament: badges of rank with variations on the fleur-de-lis, the cloth coins of merit badges pixilated with embroidery, shoulder chevrons indicating office, and backpack patches for attending camporees.

Teachers seldom fulfilled the promises implicit in school supplies: the radiance of paper, the rivery possibilities of pens, the optimism of pencil sharpeners, the usefulness of binders. But in sixth grade, Mrs. Burcalow—tiny as an elementary school student—did.

We were squirrelly sixth graders further juiced by our resentments at our stolen school and the television which—in 1971—was an aquarium of protest. We were less antiwar than pro-riot. Larry Literski made a point, now lost to history, by wearing his pajamas to school. (We were impressed.) I got into two fights with John Kendrick—fights spurred not by animosity but by a strange anxiety. Some of us talked back; some of us refused to come in from recess. At a special assembly, the boys were lined up in the gym, and our transgressions were outlined. Some boys were suspended.

Maybe because Mrs. Burcalow sensed that Kendrick and I were the ones most likely to organize misbehavior into rebellion, she encouraged us to put together what we called a class newspaper—twenty-some pages of mimeographed articles. We published a single issue. (Bonnie Neyers contributed fashion tips, which, if I remember correctly, involved chokers and platform shoes.) John and I were allowed to stay after school and work on the newspaper. Dusk was falling earlier. We worked in an empty classroom while the windows darkened. For the first time, I saw how a nameless movement in the mind becomes an idea, how an idea becomes words, how words are indented on the mimeo paper, how the mimeo paper is clamped onto a cylinder and spun, how the words are multiplied onto paper still wet with ink and fragrant with chemicals. When we were done and I stood outside, I noticed that the lights in our classroom were still on, and I saw the glowing building: the butterscotch radiances of the windows, the illuminated desks and blackboards and lights.

My zealotry for Boy Scouts led me to leadership roles. When I arrived home after being elected assistant patrol leader, I danced and squealed with the thrill of agency, the thrill of being able to plan and realize an idea.

While I sought the achieving side of Scouts, the feral side of Scouts sought me. By feral, I do not mean the wildness of camping. When I speak of the feral, I speak of the psychological, the tests and sadisms of boys being boys. Some of this I noticed only because I had been raised in such a womb of approval. I sometimes felt like Rollingstone was one large family and I was the baby. In Minnesota City, I had no such role. The older boys in the troop viewed me as comic but indulged me, and if anything, I was a leader among my peers. My sister Maureen said years later, "Colleen and I were saying that you were always kind of the CEO of your little friends." I accompanied John Kendrick on the five-mile hike required for Second Class Scouts. The test also required the applicant to prepare a meal of hamburger and potato slices baked in foil. When the meal didn't meet my standards, I flunked him. I was an eleven-year-old boy who had flunked another eleven-year-old boy. I was that guy.

So maybe it wasn't a surprise when one kid hated me. On one camping trip, he asked me if I wanted to taste a "new peanut"—actually a shell. I raised it to my mouth but hesitated when I realized it was filled with shit. He tried to force the shell in. I spat it out before I swallowed. The next year at the same camp, as I walked past his tent, he pulled his swim trunks down and crossed his legs, hiding his penis but exposing his pubic hair. "Hey, look. I'm a girl. Wanna fuck me?" This was more weird than threatening, but he continued his strange attack on me. In a drenching rain, he dug a trench around my tent. Water accumulated in this moat and began to flood my tent. That time, I started weeping. My sobs shredded the air as I tried in vain to stifle them. Tears gushed down my cheeks. I hiccupped and sniffled.

It was then that Mr. Dunn, baffled by the hatefulness of what had happened to me, apparently stepped in privately.

Mr. Dunn, our Scoutmaster, believed that boys police themselves, knew that a certain amount of teasing and clashing comes with the territory, and understood that too much protection too early would have made me into a pet. But, when he did intervene, he was taken seriously. A rumored, much-anticipated fight between John Kendrick and Jeff Brust ended before it started when Mr. Dunn simply emerged from his tent and walked toward the wood-chopping area where we had gathered to watch the fight. We dispersed. Jeff and John hung their heads and shook hands. Mr. Dunn hadn't said a word.

At any rate, my tormentor didn't attend camp the next summer.

Mr. Dunn was right to have waited. It's easy to talk about the cruelty of boys, but it's important to note the kindness of boys. When some guys decided to sprint up a hill with loaded backpacks and I, already a fat kid, fell behind, Kendrick and Paul Thicke waited for me. When canoe paddling exhausted me, Jim Dunn and Danny Valentine tactfully changed the rotation so that I rowed less often. And when Sean and Les McElmury and Mike Whetstone saw me sobbing after my tent was surrounded by a moat, they gathered around me and comforted me.

I was teased because I could be. Being the king in Rollingstone meant that I didn't know how to fend off childhood bullying.

Please note: I was not without stain: I'd thrown a knife at Sheila once; I'd locked Debby Brust in the barn during our "club" days. In high school, I would join my friends in our contempt for a few guys at the edges of our circle who acted too awkwardly, shared enthusiasms too boyishly, or even sat down at the lunch table too distinctively (arms tented, face jutting too far forward), and I would hate Elton John with what I thought was aesthetic integrity but I now realize was a putatively normal boy's spite for sissies.

But despite these once and future sins, the twelve-year-old me still radiated, *I have always been loved; I have always been encouraged; I have been raised not simply by parents but by family and village; I have seen only what children are supposed to see.* I was a piñata of innocence.

I was teased because I so clearly loved the ranks blossoming on my pockets and the badges proliferating on my sash. I loved insignia for the same reason I loved the resonant images on football helmets and the crisp type on baseball uniforms. So I never thought about what a festooned uniform is: a kind of bragging.

ON A SATURDAY NIGHT, I watched Mary Tyler Moore *with the kind of tenderness with which I had once listened to Sister Maureen. And I watched the opening credits as closely as I watched the show itself. The liquid pop-jazz guitar riff repeated; the name* Mary Tyler Moore *appeared on screen, then multiplied into a spectrum of* Mary Tyler Moores. *I saw the woman who "can turn the world on with her smile," but she wasn't smiling. I saw her through the windshield of her car. We saw the story in the wistful expressions on her face. She was leaving one place and journeying to another. She entered Minneapolis, from what appeared to be the south. Ghosted reflections in the windshield told us she had left behind people—they'd thrown her a party; they'd hugged her good-bye. In the car, approaching the city, her eyes widened and worried. She was from a smaller place and afraid of the city. She was going somewhere to make a new life.*

Then she arrived, and she was smiling. She was walking by what I would come to know as the Lake of the Isles. She was downtown near Donaldson's, where she tossed her hat into the air, and that tossed hat was crucial: outline its flight and it would resemble a skyscraper. When Mary Tyler Moore tossed her tam-o'-shanter into the air, Minneapolis became a city.

FIRE AND OTHER SOLVENTS

I NEVER EVEN FANTASIZED ABOUT BEING A PROFESSIONAL athlete. I knew from the age of six that I'd never be on a baseball card. Instead, I dreamed of being my brother, of being on a team that represented a town. When Dennis played, Rollingstone hoped and fretted and cheered.

Thanks to Little League, I got my wish. Once a week, our Minnesota City team donned our green T-shirts with white lettering and confronted a Little League team from another small town: Rollingstone, Lewiston, Stockton, or Altura. Sometimes we met them on our scruffy field behind the Minnesota City school; sometimes we traveled to their fields. We tried to carry ourselves with the shrugging grace and stoic enthusiasm of pros. Because we used the hard regulation baseball and Bobbie Barth threw true fastballs and aspiring curves, our catcher, Danny Valentine, wore the insectile gear of catcher's mask, chest protector, shin guards, globby round mitt. Bobbie and Danny really thought of themselves as a battery, a subteam with a specialized bond, and would sometimes confer on the mound like the professionals. We would sometimes join them and give advice that was way beyond our abilities: "Make them hit it on the ground; the play's at the plate." We were going through the motions, but the motions started to go through us, which felt fantastically cool.

Some of the smaller kids crouched down to shrink their strike zone and cadge walks, which made the games gummy with neurosis. Me, I swung away—maybe because our coach, John Saehler, motivated me with his very presence. John was an avid athlete: a good golfer, a first baseman on the Minnesota City men's fast-pitch softball team. He also had polio; a brace scaffolded one leg. When he batted in softball—and he was a confident, crisp line drive hitter—a runner would crouch behind the catcher and run when John hit the ball. When John played defense, he shuffled to first base for throws. As a coach, he was darkly cheerful, not given to speeches, and so without self-pity that he was virtually without self-awareness. He treated his handicap as an asterisk. And, like my dad (another athlete robbed of fluency), his presence said, *Your legs work just fine; swing away.*

At the end of the summer, our team played a tournament in Rollingstone Park. It had a real baseball field. My teammates and I looked out from the shadowy bunkers of dugouts; we followed crisp chalk baselines; we sensed our parents—who rarely attended—cheering in the bleachers; the home run fence stood hundreds of feet away. We didn't win, but we acquitted ourselves well. I stood at third, staring at the batter, starting the chatter—"Hey batter, hey batter, no batter"—with which ballplayers vent the game's anxious waiting. Then as the pitch was delivered, I tensed, ready or at least willing to stab at line drives and scoop grounders, more a goalie than a baseball fielder, ready to turn fearlessness into a surrogate for skill.

The great role model for kids standing nervously next to third base circa 1970 was Brooks Robinson of the Baltimore Orioles. I dreamed of his skill, his synapse-fast reflexes and panther acceleration, his ability to be instantly three feet in the air, his torso parallel to the ground, his body extended, his glove positioned precisely where the ball was headed, his legs and arms ready to return to a throwing stance. In the same amount of time, I would have barely turned and stabbed helplessly as the ball passed. Tim Mrozek, our shortstop, compensated for my lack of range without ever once calling me on it. He had the decency of the hyper-competent. I knew I barely deserved to be there, but I loved the game.

I especially loved being on a team that represented, however wishfully, a town. When Dennis drove for a layup as a Holy Trinity Rocket, I could feel the town leap with him—running into the Kendricks decades later, the boys would still talk about watching Dennis play—and this was as close as I would get to that blessed state.

The family continued to disperse, as families do. When I was in sixth grade, Maureen married. She calmly fanned her husband, Lowell, when he got a little light-headed at the altar. In retrospect, this seemed her droll way of waving good-bye.

Throughout that year, I knew my last connection to Rollingstone would end. Junior high waited in Winona: 1,500 kids, two buildings. The guys in my class got it into our heads that junior high was basically prison. We half expected to be bussed to a place where everyone carried shivs and your manhood was regularly insulted in the lunch line. We talked about this and thought it was kind of cool. We talked about the possibility of getting beat up because our fear was real, but we also feared losing our way in the crowd, losing our friends, and being exposed as rubes. We didn't talk about that.

In the summer that I was anticipating junior high, Dennis returned from Vietnam. I'd heard plenty about the war on the evening news, so I filtered my experience of Dennis's homecoming through what I had already heard about Vietnam vets.

I searched for wakefulness, twitchiness, moodiness, and I felt disappointed when Dennis didn't seem traumatized.

His despair was more subtle and more civil—the unease of unemployment. It was the unease of a young man who came back home to find less resonance and less possibility than he expected, and as I would find out years later, the trauma he brought back wasn't the trauma of combat. While Dennis was gone, the farm had been sold, the high school closed, the elementary school deconsecrated, and the town's Catholic culture retracted into the Sunday Mass. When Dennis returned to this erasure, he slept late. He visited friends in Rollingstone but discovered that such friendships seldom regained their momentum. Sometimes he stayed out late. There was little for him here, so one sunny August day, he packed his car and left. He drove west. Days passed. We didn't hear from him.

What is it like to drown in your own body? What is it like to feel your lungs fill and sputter? To have your heart thicken, your aortas and ventricles falter? To have your life be a tilting raft you keep slipping off of? My father knew these things—in the desperation in his capillaries, in gasps of the soft blue sacs in his lungs, and in the panic these things communicated to his brain. He was hospitalized for congestive heart failure. Fluids filled his chest cavity; his heart waded through muck. Treatment included a low-sodium diet, which he approached with the jauntiness that comes when you no longer trust doctors. When my sisters visited him in the hospital, he sent them across the street to buy him a ham and cheese sandwich and some chips.

Dennis's car trip devolved into homelessness. He spent a few nights looking through Dumpsters, scraping the pork and bean sauce out of the big restaurant cans with his finger and eating that. But he found work as an orderly in a nursing home. There, he met a woman who was thirty years old, divorced, with five kids. They fell in love and sent back news of their marriage. Soon, he began working as a driver for UPS.

One afternoon after his hospitalization, Dad sat on the bed so he could lie down and watch TV. I was sitting next to him. As he lay down, salt spilled from his pocket with the gracefulness with which sand spills through an hourglass. He winked at me.

As expected, the first days at junior high were weird, but the first day at almost anything is weird. The only Rollingstone faces I saw were Larry and Heidi Literski, and Larry was inexplicably holding court already. (Heidi was an attractive girl and thus radioactive.) When I stepped off the bus, my 1,500 new peers swarmed around me and rushed in two streams into two buildings that covered two blocks. Alone in the herd, queasy with nerves, looking for where a fight might erupt, rushing to my locker and fumbling with the combination, I found my first class, English with Mr. Rasmussen. When I got there, I saw that the kids from the bigger Winona schools knew each other. Dave Hultgren, Rick Knapik, Tom Van Diense, and Mike Campbell picked up on a conversation they'd apparently been having since first grade (only apparently—they hadn't all attended the same grade school). I left every class, reentered the stampede between rooms and buildings, and entered a new room, where I was surrounded by new students and a new teacher squinting at a new seating chart. I had no classes with my Rollingstone classmates, and Kendrick was over at one of the Catholic schools. I felt less like a human being with agency than a molecule which had been dissolved into a new solution. In that solvent, my last real connections to Rollingstone disappeared.

I visited my former neighbor Karl Herber that fall, and, when we walked up to the farm, the place had the sadness of an attic. The Herbers cultivated the fields, but they didn't need the pasture. Unchewed by cows, no longer the scene of daily Beatles movie re-creations, the grass had grown and thickened. Waist-high and nasty as rope, it obscured our landmarks and stung our legs. I had thought that the land would be more sentimental. I couldn't walk in the pasture; it was too thick. I had to wade in the stuff and grew tired.

So I visited the abandoned house. When I stepped inside, its emptiness congealed into strangeness: Dust accumulated on its sills and dirtied its windows. The water had ebbed out of the toilet, and a brown ring was left in the bottom. I didn't learn the lesson I should have learned—that the soul of a place is always imputed. I didn't feel quite what I would have felt today, which is sadness. I felt shock and prurience, as if I'd seen pictures of a tortured animal. Looking up *prurience* in the OED, I see that its root means "to itch." For days, I returned to these images—the clotted pasture, the vacant room, the brown toilet—scratching them across my mind.

Early one morning, Mom, not quite awake, received a call. The caller said, "Mrs. Fenton, your barn is burning." Outside our Minnesota City house, there was the vestigial barn we used as a garage. But when my mother hurried to the window, stretching the cord in those tethered days, that barn stood intact. The caller identified himself. It was one of the Herber boys, reporting news of the barn on our old place, the place his family owned.

The choice of pronoun—"*your* barn"—was striking. It signaled that the depth of ownership my family felt was no mere sentimental delusion, that our love for the place had somehow become a part of the place. But in another sense, our claim to the place was a sentimental delusion. We stored no hay, milked no cows, and held no deed. The pronoun gave us our barn. The fire destroyed it.

TO CELEBRATE OUR POST–GRADE school maturity, the junior high lunchroom sold ice cream sandwiches. The tough kids would spend their lunch breaks standing in the middle of the lunchroom, eating their ice cream sandwiches and conferring with each other about pressing tough-kid matters. Only in junior high could an ice cream sandwich be the mark of a badass.

The rest of us would sit more or less obediently at tables. Many of us ate the slightly more expensive "hamburger lunch," which replaced the entrée and vegetable of that day with a burger and fries. Hundreds of kids hunched protectively over their plates because if the toughs were still hungry—and since they ate only ice cream, they were—they would scan the room, pick someone out, walk up to him, and ask in a bit of sarcasm, "Hey, kid, can I borrow a fry?" The target would sometimes give up the fry; sometimes he wouldn't. Sometimes retribution would be threatened. An apocryphal story had Scott Ender, quarterback and good student, sticking a fork in the hand of one of the hoods. There seemed to have been enough supervision to prevent violence but not enough to dispel fear. Thus, lunch created solidarity as we sat, backs turned to the enemy, forks uneasily at the ready.*

*Daryl Lanz once decided to punk the pretense of *borrow*. He "borrowed" a fry and then returned it at the end of the lunch hour. Additional regional note: in Minnesota, *borrow* can also mean *lend*.

BOB NEWHARTS-IN-WAITING

ONCE IT BECAME CLEAR THAT I WOULDN'T BE BEATEN to death—this took a couple days—I noticed something about some of the guys in my classes, especially my first English class. They were verbal; they knew Marx Brothers movies; they were rowdy like all junior high kids, but there was a patter of commentary on top of their rowdiness. And they had friends who were similarly verbal, good kids whose archness never veered into insubordination, who knew and imitated and even mocked TV shows and movies and *MAD* magazine. They tried to invent a language. They may have even understood that *Batman* had been ironic.

In Rollingstone, culture was something we loved, but accepted, like a gentle snow. You laughed at Dick Martin or Red Skelton, you danced to the Beatles, but no one was a fan. We were far less likely to say, "I will memorize this and parrot it and maybe even judge it." And so in this quoting and enthusing, some new possibility fizzed.

That possibility came alive for me—and, I suspect, my new friends—in *The Bob Newhart Show.* The *Bob Newhart* theme began with Bob, outside a downtown building in another midwest-

Dad must have retained some kind of hope. Certainly, Dad didn't think that he would farm again, but maybe he hoped for an alternative to his life without work, an alternative to his life spent tending flowers, fixing the porch, and attempting leatherwork from kits. He heard of a surgeon in Washington State who might help him. He and Mom flew out to Dennis and Doris's. The day of the surgery, I was getting dressed after phys ed when the gym teacher sought me out, making his way through just-showered boys jamming their gym clothes into their tiny lockers. I was told to go to the principal's office—words that stirred fear. My gym teacher was serious but not angry, and I couldn't think of any transgressions. I said to Daryl Lanz something like, "My dad's having surgery. I hope everything's all right."

As I walked and the list of what I might have done wrong dwindled, I realized that everything was not all right. I saw Colleen, raw-eyed, standing outside by the busses. When she said, "Dad died," it was a confirmation, not a revelation.

I realize now that Dad probably died happy. My mom had wanted to buy him fresh flowers but had been rushed, so she bought yellow plastic roses from the gift shop. The flowers bloomed their plastic bloom beside him. His surgery time approached, and fear inevitably swarmed in him and emphasized the metal bed rails, the unfamiliar room, the secured TV, the blue water jugs; but he was also suffused with hope that when he awoke, everything would be changed—that he would be the vigorous man in the picture you see on the next page, taken sometime in the happy fifties; that he would again be the man who carried my mother across the dance floor; that he would again be the boy who had won a basketball tournament and was jumping into a car with his friends in that last moment of his youth; that he could enjoy at last what Wallace Stevens called the pleasures of life: the sun, the air, the joy of having a body. Then, right before the surgery, a blood clot loosened from a vein, sought his heart, and killed him.

*

ern city, with his hand on his hat. Amid the brisk, upbeat horns, the camera follows Bob as he crosses the Chicago River and navigates a landscape of concrete and bridges and trains. When Bob arrives at the end of his commute, the music calms to a piano riff, a tree appears, and the camera pans up at a new high-rise. The credits end as he kisses his pretty wife in what looked to us like a glamorous apartment. We liked the implicit promise here: plain, ironic guys can have awesome lives. We also knew there was a mandatory waiting period before you got such a life.

LEARNING TO SKATE WAS LIKE learning to ride a bike all over again: wobble, thud; wobble, thud; feeling bruises start to ooze beneath my skin. As I teetered on my ankles and used my stick like a cane, the North Stars seemed even more heroic. Skating took a basic task—standing up and walking—and made it elegant and impossible. It was as if the North Stars had taught themselves to exhale flowers.

FLOW

I BEGAN TO STUTTER. WHY DID MY PROBLEMS SPEAKING become stuttering? Why do synapses and muscles that usually work just fine seize up for no reason and humiliate you? It may simply be neurology: a 404 page in the autonomic nervous system, a clenching and failing along the pathway from formed thought to vibrating air. The mind blanches; the world is both too near and too far away. Words arrive but jam.

But stuttering feels like more than a glitch; stuttering feels like an allergic reaction to moments. As an adult, I am most likely to stutter when I am in a new situation—a new job, a new town, a new status—or when I have acted stupidly enough often enough that daily life begins to feel like a bad first date. I stutter when one screw up cascades into several and embarrassment adds up to shame. I associate it with fear. I do not stutter when I am angry. And I associate stuttering with doubt. I have never stuttered drunk because beer for me is liquid theology. And stuttering is fed by the self-centeredness of adolescence. A stutterer takes his anxiety very seriously.

My mother traced the onset of my stutter to a single moment. Maureen and her new husband, Lowell, had moved to Colorado—baffling to me that anyone would be motivated to move only by the vague sense of another place's possibilities and charisma. I would hold onto each place I have lived in for as long as I could because place holds out the best hope for connection and resonance. Mom and Dad and I flew out upon the birth of the first grandchild, Nathan.

We stepped out into a relentless not-Minnesota. Colorado's skyline was surging rock, its land brown, its air thin and dazzlingly blue. It questioned the human. After soft Minnesota, Colorado was as brutal as a moon.

Sometime during our visit, Mom and Dad agreed to watch Nathan while Maureen and Lowell and I drove up to Cripple Creek and Pikes Peak. After the chintzy dustiness of Cripple Creek, a hike in the scraggly but beautiful land seemed refreshing. As I walked, I discovered something ambiguous at first, then unmistakable: a person, a young man in blue jeans with a neat bullet hole in his head. We called the police. They cordoned off the body with yellow tape, asked a few questions of us, and let us go. What was strange was how little I thought about this in the coming months. But I began to stutter.

My stuttering will probably baffle me for as long as I live. In some ways, it feels like alcoholism—a predisposition deep in my neurons that can be activated by an embarrassingly broad spectrum of stresses from everyday social stumbles to the discovery of a dead body. It also resembles alcoholism in that it seems rooted in what I can only call an inflammation of the self. When I stutter, I do not feel a part of a tribe or the servant of a cause. Speech becomes a rope bridge to be crossed, and success means nothing more than not falling down.

Stuttering betrays a kind of spiritual homelessness in me, and in junior high, that homelessness was both literal—our barn had burned, our house had rotted, our pasture had degenerated—

and metaphorical. I'd left my Rollingstone friends but didn't quite feel as if I was a part of my new gang at junior high.

To this day, my most persistent stuttering is often associated with death, especially when I see the vacated body and I cannot escape the possibility that death always defeats the self—that we *are* and then we *are no more.* When my friend Bill Schuth died, I stuttered for two weeks afterward, and I had to think hard about my faith.

When I was in junior high, I was decades away from these insights and anything remotely resembling faith. And death wasn't done with my family.

But once again, my damaged speech had its compensations and gifts. I grasped at fluency of any sort—and if I could not have fluency in the literal sense of speaking well, I could perhaps enjoy it in its deeper sense, in the sense of its Latin root, which means "to flow." And nothing seemed more fluent to me than hockey. A complete lack of talent still seemed like an obstacle that could be overcome.

When we first moved to Minnesota City, the pond below our house was the one great promise of the new place, which otherwise seemed to offer only retreat and entropy. In winter, the pond froze, so water suddenly had the smoothness and possibility of a page.

When the sky was still bruised with dawn, I would lace my smooth-bladed hockey skates and totter out our back door to the woods that descended to the backwater. I would slide down the hill, leaning against it and dragging my hockey stick in the snow to slow myself, sometimes grabbing a tree to brake myself. At the bottom, I crunched across snow-crusted weeds and then, more precariously, stepped across the snow-covered ice. The ice was usually uneven, sometimes bumpy when snow fell and melted and refroze, sometimes veined with cracks left by the tectonic shifting in the pond. John Kendrick and Paul Thicke and Jeff Brust and I scrimmaged and ran impromptu drills. We reenacted game situations. We imagined ourselves moving in a choreographed squadron in the manner of the NHL players we idolized, shuffling the puck on our sticks, adjusting our positions. We worked on capturing the scooping, satisfying force of the backhand; the choreography of passing; the deft ballistics of wrist shots; the simplifying speed of slap shots. We got so we could raise the puck, and the game became a little more dangerous and a little more fun.

We played for hours. Sometimes we would even skate at night, after it was too late to see the puck but we could still see to skate. I have never thought much about what Dad did while I spent my days on the ice, about how much time he spent in an empty house in winter.

I loved hockey at any time and in any form. Back on the farm, Mom and Dad had given me what might have been the coolest Christmas present ever: a tabletop hockey set equipped with twelve sets of silk-screened tin players representing teams of the NHL. You pushed and pulled and wiggled the controls to make the men skate; you spun the plastic tips of the rods to make the players shoot or pass. The little men with the unchanging faces lurched up and down the rink, then spun like dervishes.

I started a league with my friends. I was the green and gold North Stars. I think Thicke was the magenta and navy Canadiens, Kendrick the black and yellow of the Boston Bruins. Thicke won. I was a competent player, but what the game really indulged was my passion for creating and organizing, an entrepreneurial and artistic spark that kept looking for kindling in the oddest places. I gave names to teams. I scheduled tournaments and recorded them, and when I did those things, I created a private universe, with private heroisms and defeats, all of which I marked down on paper where it became something not quite private. When I recorded my thoughts, they subtly expanded.

DAD BOUGHT A YEAR-OLD Chevy Impala, the nicest car he had ever owned. It was big and red with a whisper of the finned generosity of sixties car design. It had automatic windows, which couldn't have fascinated us more if we'd been chimpanzees. When the remaining family drove to church, he would light up cigars in it, even in winter when the windows could not be rolled down. None of us really minded, although we coughed and sputtered in the backseat because we could not bear to ruin this one moment of patriarchal glory. I would later discover that he had struck a deal with the car dealership. There would be no payments for one year. I don't know if this was a sign of his hope for the future or a sense of what was about to happen.

THE LAST DAYS OF BOYHOOD

EIGHTH GRADE IS A UNIQUE EMOTIONAL WASTELAND. The play of childhood has stopped, but the passions of adolescence haven't started. I was no longer wandering in pastures, or pasting pictures of exotic animals in books, or loitering on the lawn until games that vaguely resembled baseball formed around me, or riding bikes for the sake of riding bikes. I was a few years away from discovering music and literature. Sex surged inside me but took the form of embarrassing wet dreams, furtive masturbation, and stuttery crushes—and a lot of good that did me. I was years away from finding my Suzanne Pleshette in my urban apartment. Sports and Scouts were fizzling. And so I spent a lot of time in a junky, jumpy world—reading *MAD* magazine, immersing myself in *Star Trek* reruns, and, with my buddy Gary Mahaffey, lighting Hai Karate on fire just to see what would happen. Junior high seemed a prolonged avoidance of emotion.

* * *

My parents were assumed annoyances, like alarm clocks. I didn't know what they thought about.

* * *

Dad must have retained some kind of hope. Certainly, Dad didn't think that he would farm again, but maybe he hoped for an alternative to his life without work, an alternative to his life spent tending flowers, fixing the porch, and attempting leatherwork from kits. He heard of a surgeon in Washington State who might help him. He and Mom flew out to Dennis and Doris's. The day of the surgery, I was getting dressed after phys ed when the gym teacher sought me out, making his way through just-showered boys jamming their gym clothes into their tiny lockers. I was told to go to the principal's office—words that stirred fear. My gym teacher was serious but not angry, and I couldn't think of any transgressions. I said to Daryl Lanz something like, "My dad's having surgery. I hope everything's all right."

As I walked and the list of what I might have done wrong dwindled, I realized that everything was not all right. I saw Colleen, raw-eyed, standing outside by the busses. When she said, "Dad died," it was a confirmation, not a revelation.

I realize now that Dad probably died happy. My mom had wanted to buy him fresh flowers but had been rushed, so she bought yellow plastic roses from the gift shop. The flowers bloomed their plastic bloom beside him. His surgery time approached, and fear inevitably swarmed in him and emphasized the metal bed rails, the unfamiliar room, the secured TV, the blue water jugs; but he was also suffused with hope that when he awoke, everything would be changed—that he would be the vigorous man in the picture you see on the next page, taken sometime in the happy fifties; that he would again be the man who carried my mother across the dance floor; that he would again be the boy who had won a basketball tournament and was jumping into a car with his friends in that last moment of his youth; that he could enjoy at last what Wallace Stevens called the pleasures of life: the sun, the air, the joy of having a body. Then, right before the surgery, a blood clot loosened from a vein, sought his heart, and killed him.

*

I cried once, having maintained my composure throughout the food-clotted day of his death and the awkward wake and the funeral where my friends Paul Thicke and Greg Bingold served Mass and Paul read one of the liturgies. Colleen broke down as the casket was wheeled away, but I didn't. As we were walking down the aisle and as we were almost to the back of the church, I looked up briefly and saw my Boy Scout troop, at attention, in uniform. Mr. Dunn had arranged for everyone to show up. Sobs loosened in me and didn't quiet until I was in the car.

I almost cried a second time when, upon returning to homeroom English, the class presented me with a goalie's stick. Kevin Poblocki, fellow inhabitant of the junior high lunch table, had told them about my almost private passion for the game.

I did not cry again for my father, and I did not feel sad. I envied my brother, who, as a Vietnam veteran, could weep at the casket without seeming like a sissy. But I otherwise resented people who could grieve properly, those for whom grief was a richness recalled, who wept unashamedly, whose gestures were graceful with loss. When a classmate wrote about his father's death in simple language, I thought he was playacting to get attention. I hated my grief. I hated its staticky banality.

My father's death placed awful burdens on my mom. Until then, the time in Minnesota City had been a respite for her. She had still worked full time, but she no longer moved with the franticness of a woman who also needed to see that a farm was operating and that five kids were where they were supposed to be. But even though she had to suddenly raise a teenage son alone, she could not stop working. She later told me that she said to herself, maybe in prayer, that she hoped that she had raised me well because she had to trust me from here on out. Because she had no choice, she'd trusted Dennis to run the farm when he was fourteen. Compared to that, not much was expected of me. I was simply to stay out of trouble.

*

I don't remember much about the year that followed my father's death. A few facts remain: Mom worked five days a week, some of them nights, leaving about 2:30 in the afternoon and arriving home at about midnight.

Now, when I think of how I experienced my father's death, I cut myself a little slack. Junior high—the sugar-fueled darting, the fact that I was too old to cry and too young to weep, the sensibility stranded between Seuss and Shakespeare—left me with little but wisecracks and a desire not to cry. Culture rehearses emotion, and I had no culture adequate to grief: *MAD* magazine makes an awful Kaddish.

Even if she had been around more, I felt for my mother the magnetic repulsion that boys of that age feel for their mothers. So if I were to sag and sob, who would have caught me?

I did feel my father's loss, but in a way I have only recently understood. Death was a desiccant. I knew enough theology to know that God is everywhere, and I understood the implication of this: the same God who had tortured and taken my father suffused the walls, the curtains, the linoleum. The weeks after Dad died were the glittering remainder of May, and as I got off the school bus, the house appeared as it would to any other junior high boy whose parents had gone away for a while—it was a treasure I could explore and exploit, maybe nefariously. But when I opened the door, the sunlight outside darkened the shadow inside the house. When I visited Karl Herber, I'd seen our abandoned farmhouse. I knew that human presences hide the indifference of things, their silence and stillness. So when I got home, I threw my books on the table. I ate Oreos, cake swampy with milk, and processed cheese sandwiches on white bread. I flipped on the TV and enjoyed its toxic companionship. Being fourteen, I cranked the tunes. Mom wouldn't be home for seven hours.

III WINONA

FATHERS AND FRIENDS

ABOUT THOSE TUNES I WAS CRANKING. THAT SUMMER, which was spikily, inappropriately sunny, I spent hours in my friend Gary's house down at the far end of the road where the houses had the quaintness of Monopoly houses, and where we could see the river from his window, and listened to dungeony Black Sabbath, messy Cheech and Chong, and Alice Cooper. Alice Cooper is what resonated; his music excoriated without scarring. It was punk at the edges but bubblegum in the middle—a mixture you could appreciate for only about two weeks at a certain age—but it wasn't fake. "School's Out" said that, while we did attend school, we sure were glad it was out. "I'm Eighteen" was an anthem of youthful rebellion sung by someone who was legally an adult. "No More Mr. Nice Guy" tells the story of a kid who used to be sweet and who still *goes to church,* albeit with a bad attitude. This wasn't rebellion; it was conformity with a caveat. It was not music that Gary and I would listen to much in high school. My tastes went toward the Rolling Stones, the Allman Brothers, and Steely Dan. Gary's went more toward the blue-collar rock of Bob Seger and ZZ Top, and he would take up guitar. Decades later, I would see his band in a bar in Winona and realize that he'd kept the faith and had practiced all these years.

There was something in that laughable snot-rock. The guitars moved with more freedom and less self-deprecation than the lyrics. In its cartoony way—and I was only three or four years from watching Saturday morning cartoons—the music of Alice Cooper suggested that anger could be the stuff of songs. It was gateway art.

In ninth grade, dropping off an assignment in a journalism class, I spied some assignments done by the same teacher's creative writing class. On top was a poem. If you were to assign a computer to write a poem representative of bright, sensitive youth in 1974, it would have come up with something like this:

I sit
Under a tree
And wonder
Why there is war.

Yet what I noticed was the poem's slight artfulness, the near rhymes that felt like completed passes, the line breaks that feinted like curve balls. For the first fourteen years of my life, I'd been an articulate monkey—and so had my friends: taunting, joking, boasting, trading, planning, mimicking, mocking, interrupting, cheering, parroting, chattering, gossiping, coordinating, complaining, inciting, and yelling. But this was different. This little poem caught and turned a gear in me: however silly, at its core was introspection, a productive private stillness. Someone I knew had done this, and I could do it, too. At that point, all of the energy I had spent recording sports in my Vikings Book and creating little newspapers found a new, deeper outlet. I started to write poetry and song lyrics.

* * *

"Idle hands are the devil's workshop" sounds like one of those clucky, small-souled sayings that have become aphorisms through sheer meanness. But sometimes you know you need to act, to board a bus, to agree to be somewhere, to learn something new, and you know that, if this doesn't dissipate the pain, at least it keeps it from congealing even more horribly. So I signed up for a summer school debate class at the senior high. Mom and I both thought it was a good idea.

As it turned out, the satisfactions of debate were in many ways the satisfactions of my 1960s childhood. The senior high still smelled of new construction, of compounds and pastes, and I liked that smell. It invigorated me. It was the smell of school supplies, of the fragrant plastic of the *Britannica Junior* bindings and the Fright Factory goop. It was the smell of the future, which, in the early seventies, still had some of the utopian romance of flying cars and apartments on stalks in the sky.

I loved debate for many reasons. It was the summer of the Watergate hearings, and debaters—guys with notes and outlines—were almost celebrities. Unlike classes, debate was a mental activity that was not judged primarily by obedience. Like my baseball card hobby in grade school, it rewarded accumulation. You had to clip the quotations from the research guides and paste them on index cards with the fragrant glue sticks and write them on index cards and file them in metal boxes and even read articles on your own and build a case. I wrote to Senator Mondale, who sent me big envelopes of background material. You got to think the thoughts of a president. But you also got to cut and paste like a boy, and I think I needed that retreat into boyhood.

* * *

A year after Dad died, Mom and I moved into a smaller house in Winona. Unlike the traumatic move from the farm to Minnesota City, this move was undramatic and, if we hadn't been somehow saying good-bye to Dad, almost cheery. We picked the place together, a small house with a bedroom for me off the kitchen. Mom understood that my bedroom needed a little extra privacy—not because there would be girls in it (I wish) but because that was where my fatherless self would go all Hamlet.

As odd as it may sound to more sophisticated people, Winona felt like a city, in Greil Marcus's sense of a city: a circuit of possibilities. I could walk to movies. I could walk to libraries and colleges and a record store and a bookstore. I was closer to my new Winona friends.

It was also a staging area for a search I didn't even know I was undertaking: the search for fathers and brothers.

* * *

Ever since my dad had died, I'd felt like a human pinball. A clueless kid who was experiencing emotions he couldn't feel and a loss he could neither grasp nor grieve, I needed all the help I could get.

Burnell Manley was the senior high debate coach. He was less small than compact, booming, freckled, effervescent, red-haired, mischievous, a burly leprechaun. He was short—so short that it was the first thing you noticed about him—but large-chested, with a lavish tattoo of a sailing ship on his chest that we could sometimes see through his shirt. We discovered he had been in the Marines. I knew from Dennis that Marines were tough but not necessarily mean.

That summer after my dad died, our summer school class debated whether gays should be allowed to adopt children. While I was glazing my gut opposition to gay adoption with legitimate arguments about traditions and stability and the best interests of the child and looking out at my classmates, self-consciousness percolated into panic, constricting my throat and baffling my brain. A need to show off spritzed through me, and I blurted out, "Do you want your children raised by . . . sissies?" It may have been the single dumbest sentence I've ever uttered.

As hate speech, this was pretty lame, although if there were any gays in the audience, they knew that *sissy* meant *fag*. Was I sickly trying to impress Wanda Schlesser, who had nobly taken the pro-adoption side? Was it the rhetorical equivalent of pulling her ponytails? Was I trying to make it clear that, even though I was at best a mediocre athlete and maybe something of a nerd, I was not queer, so please beat up someone else? I hated Elton John and kept my distance from the less easily dismissed David Bowie for the same reason. Was it the nastiness of all speech uttered when its targets are apparently not in the room—not in the room and, as far as we knew, not in the world? Gays were cartoons. I might as well have said, "Would you want your kids raised by the Flintstones, with their foot-powered cars and birds for appliances?"

If I were to hear a kid say anything similar today, my contempt would be undisguised. Mr. Manley let it pass despite the fact that my intolerance offended his beliefs, and I think he was wise to do so. It wasn't that he avoided conflict. In conservative Winona, he had a bumper sticker on his car that said, "Don't Blame Me—I Voted for McGovern." He argued against the overwhelming consensus of debate coaches in the state who thought debate was a matter of rattling off as many arguments as possible. He insisted that debate descended from rhetoric and that not simply the speed but the shape of the argument mattered. He was not training us to win tournaments but to be effective adults who could stand up in front of people and communicate with them. These weren't dramatic moral standoffs. But they showed me a first glimpse of how real grown-ups could function in the world of policy and opinion and culture.

I think Mr. Manley knew that my spasm of hatred would pass, that I was a combustible kid whose father had died less than two months before. Mr. Manley died in August 2004 of a heart attack on a sailboat in Key West, Florida, where he had retired. His obituary reminded me that he was a judo black belt. He'd let my stupidity dissipate, knowing that if he countered it, it would flare and solidify. He was a sailor—a "self-taught mathematical navigator"—and sailors know how to tack. He knew that living a principled life meant ongoing forgiveness. Ten years after I'd spewed that invective, when—after a horrible night late in law school—I first realized that I might be an alcoholic, he was the first person I called.

In some ways, Mr. Manley was more a father figure than my actual dad. I know I sometimes was disciplined at home, but Dad couldn't ever show me how to act in the world because it seemed he didn't really know himself. He was too resentful to work well with others and too sick to work well by himself. I loved my dad, and he was an engaging and decent man, but I never looked to him for *guidance.* Mr. Manley imposed goofy punishments for our goofy crimes. For basic classroom misbehavior, we would have to sit in the "green chair," which meant leaning with your back against the wall with your legs bent as if in a chair, supporting yourself with your quivering quadriceps. But more serious transgressions—those that hurt other human beings—received not a traditional punishment but the kind of stern, honest talk that was far more uncomfortable than the green chair. When we made serial fun of Wanda Schlesser, who made the mistake of being both pretty and nice, the girls were excused from the room, and the boys who did this were spoken to with a chill that left us ashamed and then chastened. We were told not that we had broken a rule but that we had hurt someone. That was enough. Like Mr. Dunn, he knew how to invoke our best selves—and then he let our best selves shame our brat selves. As an adult, I will sometimes think, "What would Mr. Manley do?"

* * *

Neal Nixon, from junior high debate, gave a presentation in tenth-grade American history on the blues. He even demonstrated a blues progression. Those chords resonated in me in ways Neal never could have predicted.

We were in the five-year, post-*Tommy* window when the term *rock opera* could be said without giggling. Inspired by the poem on the junior high teacher's desk, I'd spent the summer writing poems. My poems were frustrated song lyrics. And they had accumulated into a rock opera that, thankfully, I cannot remember, although I do remember that I wrote it in longhand in a green spiral Smead notebook with no thought as to how to set it to music. I thought that Neal might help me.

We met at a pizza place near Winona State, about three blocks from my house and about the same from Neal's. It was the kind of chilled Minnesota night I've always associated with getting things started, and the place glowed the way that the Rollingstone school had glowed on that fall night four years earlier as John Kendrick and I had finished our newspaper. The smell of baking pizza drifted into the air, greeting me.

Inside at a booth, Neal, being cool, ordered coffee and lit a cigarette. Being uncool, I ordered a pop.

I wanted Neal to look at my lyrics, declare their genius, and say he would write the music for the opera. He didn't. He didn't reject them, either. Instead, he told a story.

His dad had worked for the railroad, and on weekends, Neal would be put on the train, which he could ride for free. He would ride down to St. Louis and back, reading *Huckleberry Finn*. After his dad died, when Neal was in sixth grade and he had read *Huckleberry Finn* so often that he could recite the entire first chapter by heart, he'd reverted to comic books. His older brother, who was then in law school, saw him with a comic book, yanked it from his hand with the diplomacy of an older brother, and gave him history's briefest tutorial: "Don't read that crap. Read this." He then handed him copies of Hemingway, Steinbeck, Fitzgerald, Faulkner, Hawthorne, Melville, and Thoreau. He basically dumped an American literature course on his head. In telling me this, Neal was tactfully avoiding the quality of my lyrics—and also maybe avoiding the onerous task of composing an opera as a favor to a near-stranger. But he was also making a point: what we were talking about here—this opera scribbled on a back-to-school supply—was part of a tradition.

This was more of a revelation to me than it should have been. In one sense, my family was deeply cultured. My memories of growing up are saturated with the richness of Catholicism and the buoyancy of pop culture, with the retorts of *Laugh-In* and the responses of the rosary, with the songs of the Beatles, with the brightnesses of baseball cards. But our lives in Rollingstone were empty of the things conventionally associated with culture: the civilizing oceans of symphonies, the jeweled horizons of movies. There were no museums with rooms as suggestive as encyclopedias. I had never experienced the dual citizenship of the novel.

My family didn't even look very closely at pop culture. The Beatles seemed so new because we knew nothing of their rockabilly and R and B antecedents. With his presentation on the blues, Neal acknowledged that rock music—like American literature—flowed from something, responded to something, judged itself by something in its past.

That said, my cultural ignorance wasn't entirely a bad thing. I think I had a more electric sense of possibility than someone who had grown up in a world forested with classics.

There's a fair amount of sentimental glop that surrounds the ideas of fathers and tradition. And this glop misses the tensions between father and sons, the goofinesses of fathers, the cluelessness of kids, the often half-assed ways traditions are transmitted, the sheer oppressiveness of being in a soft-focus commercial for Learning the Ancient Ways. Glop acknowledged, Neal's brother had, in the absence of a father, passed something on to Neal, and Neal had passed it on to me. Even the rebels we loved acknowledged artistic fathers. Ken Kesey praised Faulkner and Hemingway. Keith Richards worshipped Muddy Waters and Howlin' Wolf and Robert Johnson and Chuck Berry. And we worshipped Ken Kesey and Keith Richards. Starting that night over a cheese pizza, coffee, and Coke, Neal taught me that being a man meant serving a tradition. It is no accident that Neal's best friend became a novelist and that his son is a gifted jazz saxophonist.

That pizza place* would become a hangout for all my friends, and the place lives in my mind with some of the delicate thickness of montage. That place, whose only gestures to culture were the presence of Captain and Tennille's "Love Will Keep Us Together" and the Commodores' "Brick House" on the jukebox, now seems retouched with Hemingway's "A Clean, Well-Lighted Place" and Hopper's *Nighthawks*. I sought the places in Winona that reminded us of the music I liked: the railroad tracks, the boathouses on the Mississippi, Ruth's Diner, the old streets at night, and, as soon as I could sneak into them, the city's many corner bars. The goal was to absorb as much of Winona's resonance as possible, and this felt, strangely, like a quest—that is, if hanging around, drinking, listening to records, and wisecracking can be a quest.

Winona itself would become a father figure, if that makes any sense. In high school, I noted the fathers of girls I admired: Liz and Celia Henderson's dad was Tom Henderson, an MIT-trained engineer who ran a local company. He was famous among those of my friends who related a little too much to Bob Newhart for getting a perfect score on the SATs. When I was tagging along, visiting his office on some youth group fund-raising call, my friend said, "I heard you were a racquetball star."

Mr. Henderson replied, "No, I'm a racquetball . . . enthusiast."

This made him the first person I ever saw search for a word and thus the first person who ever demonstrated that words are worth searching for. But I also picked up something larger: Tom Henderson viewed business as a form of service, and service

---

*The name of the place was Papa John's. But it wasn't the national chain.

was a form of love. I sensed that Tom Henderson was proud of the products he made and the people he employed. That sense of what business could be has always stayed with me, and it has survived numerous counterexamples, including Ken Lay, Donald Trump, and the American securities industry.

Molly Murphy's dad was Leo Murphy, a partner in the town's best law firm and the son of a judge. My image of Leo Murphy became fused with Faulkner's Gavin Stevens and with Faulkner himself. I got the idea that a lawyer could do more than simply live in a town like Winona; he could understand its most fragile secrets and serve its greatest purposes.

Anita Johnson's dad was Lowell Johnson. He taught calculus at the high school. He had earned a PhD in mathematics. My friends who took his class spoke of him with a respect they afforded no other teacher. This sardonic, traditional man was the first person to embody e. e. cummings's definition of a great teacher as a predicate utterly in love with his subject. Thinking back on the influence of these men—who may not have even known I existed—it's daunting and encouraging to realize how a good life can resonate in ways you can't predict with people you may never even meet.

But not everyone I admired in Winona was a patriarch. People dropped out and lived in boathouses. People were entrepreneurial in ways that made my small world more interesting. They started bookstores where they would explain how Ginsberg descended from Whitman and record stores that smelled of patchouli oil and where you sometimes bought records simply because you liked what you heard when you walked into the store. They started plucky hippie cafés. People lived lives of seriousness and scope—the kind of lives that the nuns in Rollingstone had lived and encouraged us to live.

Everyone seems to have their own Winona. The town was a beacon of innocence, the earthly incarnation of Mayberry; it was a comic opera where they broadcast fireworks on the radio; it was a stifling, passive-aggressive purveyor of midwestern bourgeois judgment; it was a town of white trash bullies; it was a laid-back river town that provided welcome relief from the intensity of Chicago or the oppressiveness of some prairie village. But, for me, Winona suggested what I might be. Winona was my career counselor.

It was a good thing I was embracing Winona. The first place I loved would soon be erased.

* * *

During my sophomore year in high school, Sheila got married in Rochester. It was very different from Maureen's and Colleen's weddings, both of which had been parties thrown by my parents in Minnesota City and which gathered our world—relatives, friends from Rollingstone—around us. This was an event we were attending, not hosting, in a Rochester hotel, on a weeknight.

To get there, we traced the route we took so many times to see Dad in the hospital, so our family was already feeling attenuated and disconnected at the start of the night. It was the first wedding that Dad would not attend. It was a spring night, with the sun thickening toward gold at sunset. Mom, Colleen, Colleen's husband, Tom, and I were in the car, and we decided, for old times' sake, to drive through Rollingstone and then past the farm. None of us had seen it since I had visited Karl Herber in seventh grade. The lilacs might be out.

The hill seemed smaller than before and its curve less drastic. Before we knew it, we were ascending past Frank Speltz's cow pond and past the tangle of woods on the higher reaches of the hill. As we reached the top, we noticed that the Herbers had erected a white machine shed on what had been our land. This didn't surprise us. They were always improving their places. The curve of the road, the slight tug of remembered g-force, the familiar sky above the familiar fields, the innocence of the May twilight all prompted in my mind the snapshot of our farmhouse, which I had seen thousands of times and remembered thousands more. I then looked for the confirmation of its humble white classicalism, for the refreshing of memory and the reaffirming of detail that are the point of such nostalgic drives. But my eyes stumbled when they looked: there was sky where there shouldn't be sky, the sight of land tumbling into pasture, and, a fractional second later, I saw a new ranch house where our house had stood. Colleen gasped. It was as if someone had replaced a tombstone with a microwave.

And at that moment, Rollingstone and all it represented stopped being a living part of my life and became something else, a memory. Even though two of the people who had lived on that farm sat in the car with me, and I would see another in an hour, I knew that our reunion would be temporary. *I liked those humans. I am sad they are gone.*

BACK IN ROLLINGSTONE, LONG after we had left, my parents' friends Hudsy and Sylvia Hengel erected a signpost with arrows and mile markers pointing to each of their thirteen distant children.

HIPPIES FOR GERALD FORD

LIKE MOST TEENAGERS, MY INNER LIFE WAS A WEIRD combination of passionate quests and crazy detours. Around the time Neal and I started hanging out in high school, I discovered the 1973 essay collection *One Lord, One Faith, One Cornbread* while browsing in Northern Lights Books in Winona. The spiritual center of the world of *One Lord, One Faith, One Cornbread* was a collection of houses near Stanford called Perry Lane, where the novelist, LSD enthusiast, and astral entrepreneur Ken Kesey; his wife, Faye; the psychologist Vic Lovell; and some hangers-on lived in the early sixties.

Lovell and Kesey spent time "reading, writing, painting, going to graduate school and creating happenings of various kinds." Some of their younger, female hangers-on preferred "screwing, blowing pot, and reading comic books." Occasionally, they'd get "decked out and stoned in preparation for a peace march or a protest against the House Un-American Activities Committee." They were hippies before anybody used the term.

I understood the writing part of what they were doing. I was typing poems on my electric typewriter on my mom's kitchen table—bad, ersatz Dylan, Rimbaud wannabe stuff, but serious in its way. But the rest of the lifestyle posed problems. I was to become a belated, ambivalent, and, to the extent that such a thing is even possible, *incompetent* hippie.

First, there was the little problem of drugs. I had *somehow managed to have a bad trip on grass.* Yes, I was that lame. And by "a bad trip," I mean a pervasive molecular sense that the world was sinister and that I was absolutely alone, a despair it took me days to shake. All of philosophy's doubts—Zeno's fear that we can never touch each other, Descartes's fear that the world is a joke, Plato's fear that we stumble through a cave—soaked through me.

Then there was the problem of politics. Those California dreamers certainly had some shades to their politics—some were more communitarian, others more libertarian, some more radical, some more incremental—but I detected a unifying distrust of American power and disdain for American business. Pretty much none of them shared my emerging enthusiasm for Gerald Ford.

A friend of mine recently pointed out that "Hippies for Ford" is pretty much the definition of cognitive dissonance. But it didn't seem so at the time. My adolescence—like, I suspect, many people's—was a series of internships in different belief systems. As I was doing a little dropping out and smoking dope, I was also putting together a take on politics that I later learned might be described as Burkean but was probably less about its intellectual antecedents—I was years from reading Burke and am just now reading him thoroughly—and more about how Gerald Ford seemed like a good guy and how the student radicals who blew up buildings in Madison seemed like complete dicks. It was a philosophy built on gratefulness and pragmatism and the realization that the government did much to ensure my security and that business did much to create my prosperity. Such thinking would not have played well on Perry Lane, especially my enthusiasm for business. But that enthusiasm was undeniable. Decades later, when I saw Cyril Connolly's phrase "the adrenalin of commerce," I thought, *Yes, that captures my love of business.*

And, finally, there was the problem of a supporting cast. Lovell and Kesey and their fellow *One Lord, One Faith, One Cornbread* contributors could count on a certain camaraderie. I'm not just talking about the free love portion of the lifestyle that was both *immensely appealing* to my fifteen-year-old self and *completely hypothetical.* (To put this in Venn diagram terms, "Girls Who Showed an Interest in Me" and "Teenage Winona Hippies" were both fairly modest sets. Their intersection was empty.) Vaguely druidic happenings and free-form dance moments required girls. Being a hippie was a group activity.

I did find a few sympathetic friends. There was no shortage of guys willing to smoke dope, laugh disproportionately at *Welcome Back, Kotter* and *Hogan's Heroes,* and agree that much of adult society was bullshit. But my hippie phase didn't last long.

The thing is, the hippies themselves seemed to have moved on. *One Lord, One Faith, One Cornbread* had the feel of an elegy. Published in 1973, it was more memoir than manifesto.

The collection's world view was probably simply too utopian: it assumed a gentleness, an honesty, and a trust that human beings can't deliver. As Vic Lovell touchingly wrote, "It seems to me that the most important assumption which underlies the current insurgencies is the Enlightenment belief that we can be much better than we are." As a philosophy, it never quite accounted for the darker parts of human nature.

Or, like many such movements, the hippies accounted for our darker impulses by dividing humanity into angels and demons. Those of us who view all humans—whether they spend their days in a commune or a boardroom—as mixtures of good and evil find such movements hard to fully accept and prone to horrible abuses of trust.

A whole bunch of vulnerable, ostentatiously seeking people who discount their own capacity for evil are a cult waiting to happen. I don't think it's any accident that one of the first true hippie scenes—Ken Kesey and the Merry Pranksters—had a megalomaniac, a charismatic jock, at its center. Fortunately for the Pranksters, Kesey appeared to be that rarest of beings—a fundamentally decent megalomaniac. When the charismatic leader was less decent, all sorts of awful things happened.

I don't know how I sensed these darker tendencies in high school. I just had a vague sense that the guys a few years older than us—most of whom took on the outward signs of the counterculture—were jerks in the way that big brothers are often jerks. (As noted earlier, Dennis was so much older than me, he was more like an uncle.) But I knew that, with a few exceptions, I would never quite trust male hippies.*

While I rejected much of *One Lord, One Faith, One Cornbread*'s version of the sixties, I was surprised at how much sympathy I still had with these people. But the most important thing the hippies did was so simple and vulnerable, it embarrassed me. They felt their emotions. They were kind to each other. They searched for the deepest truths.

I was even more surprised to realize that, while I thought I was rebelling against the adult world, I was in fact reclaiming its deepest values. The sisters of Holy Trinity had long since dispersed. My mother was, of necessity, too busy making a living to spend a lot of time hanging out with me in those years. But

---

* Steve Jobs was another one of those messianic types. For the most part, Jobs used his grandiose tendencies for good. But it's important to note that an exquisite design sense doesn't equal enlightenment—fascists are often wonderful designers. And, as becomes clear in Walter Isaacson's biography, Jobs was remarkably cruel. When he went to Reed College, he actively studied a charismatic student drug dealer and commune leader who would use stares and other forms of intimidation to gain power over people. Later in his career, Jobs would bully callow engineers by asking them, "Have you dropped acid? Are you a virgin?" He used the openness and experimentation and trust associated with the sixties—the uptightness of the fifties at least gave people some boundaries—as openings to gain power over people. And, I'd suggest, that kind of misses the point.

the values those women had taught me as a child—*accept people for what they are, ignore the superficial, money doesn't matter but work does, be modest and mindful, take responsibility for the effects of your actions on God's creation, seek truth*—were the durable core of what the residents of Perry Lane had to offer. But I don't think I was subtle or smart enough to see that at the time.

* * *

But one aspect of the sixties seemed completely vital, and it shapes my life to this day. And that was rock music.

Unlike hippie culture, the music I listened to wasn't peaceful, it wasn't benign, it wasn't pastoral, and despite its yearnings, it never assumed that we could be much better than we were.

First and foremost, it was *music*. You could fully immerse yourself in those big sounds and alchemized words. All I had to do was retreat to my room and listen to records in that strange state that is one part meditation, one part frenzy. I stood there among dirty clothes and records that I let clutter the floor, in that annex that looked out through small windows onto our backyard, listening to records on our ninety-nine-dollar JC Penney stereo. The cheap stereo was fine with me. I know from hearing Neal Nixon (and later my wife) point out nuances in music, which I would never have picked out on my own, that a better stereo would have been lost on me. I listened for structure and hook and insistence and beat and words. I listened for the kind of energy that can push through even a car radio. I listened like a beer drinker—music was a vague wash that took me to a place where I felt more deeply at home. I didn't dance, precisely, but I did something. I would have been embarrassed if someone had entered the room.

The Stones got right what the utopians at Perry Lane got wrong: evil is inside us. With songs such as "Paint It, Black," "Sway," "No Expectations," "Stray Cat Blues," "Monkey Man," "Jumpin' Jack Flash," and "Brown Sugar," they created a slightly diabolical, subtly sexualized world that I inhabited without ever quite thinking it had anything to do with me. (In real life, I was chubby and awkward.) Of all the rock bands, they most successfully managed to capture what they loved about the blues and merge it with what they had lived through in the sixties—the dislocations of drugs, the abyss of Brian Jones's "death by misadventure." "Sway" pictured a day which fractured in your mind before it even began, a hangover that felt like a crack the devil could sneak into. Like most bluesmen, the Stones believed in the Devil.

But there was one risk the Stones were unwilling to take. They were never uncool. They never showed how much all this mattered.

For that, I had the Who.

Pete Townshend was born uncool. Just look at that nose. That windmilling guitar playing was the opposite of the Keith Richards/Joe Perry cool guitarist prototype. He hadn't lost his father, but he played guitar like he did. (If you view guitar playing as barely concealed sex, you feel for the poor women Townshend came into contact with.) Townshend was neither languid nor laconic, neither confident nor nuanced. I admired the Stones. But I loved Pete Townshend. My protruding gut distanced me from the suave Stones but aligned me with the cloddish Who. A huge schnoz, a belly—either way, as Townshend sang in *Quadrophenia*, we were both punks with stutters.

The Who was a seventies band that accidentally formed in the sixties. While I know that those early Who records are beloved by many, they strike me as tinny and often jokey. ("Happy Jack"? Seriously?*) The band didn't figure out what they were about until the rock opera *Tommy*. Granted, *rock opera* is a silly term. But it gave Pete Townshend the space to create the art

---

*Evidently the age you are when you encounter music really matters. A friend of mine with exceptional taste listens to the early Who and hears the first punk band. He is four years older than me, and those years make all the difference.

that was inside of him, and that art wasn't AM rock singles circa 1967. Townshend reached not just for ecstasy but for meaning. And to do that, you need a big canvas. In *Tommy* and *Who's Next* and, especially, *Quadrophenia,* he found it.

It's easy to dismiss the seventies as pretentious—and in the case of much ersatz Tolkien prog rock, it was—but in the case of Townshend the charge isn't true because he wasn't pretending. The lyrics are surprisingly grounded, especially in *Quadrophenia.* Fried eggs that make you sick first thing in the morning, haircuts and motorbikes, eel pie, a mom and dad who are "really all right": it's all a long way from the pompous non sequiturs of, say, "Stairway to Heaven." Even the messianic Tommy played pinball, the most trivial and teenage of skills. But the music is big. Listen to the weirdly knuckley keyboards of "Baba O'Riley," Daltrey's muscular vocals in the verse, and Townshend's ethereal ones in the chorus; and on "Sea and Sand" the drums as inventive as guitars and the guitars as violent as drums. There's a storminess fueled by half-understood anger and a confused yearning for something more sublime. The Who inhabited a very special place that no other band—not the Beatles or Stones, the Byrds or Creedence, Zevon or Springsteen, the Sex Pistols or the Clash, the Replacements or U2*—ever quite occupied: that place where anger ferments into transcendence. And the seventies gave the Who the room they needed to make this music: double albums, big stadium stages, a willingness to take the spiritual seriously, and lasers.

Neal and I managed to get tickets to the Who's show at the St. Paul Civic Center. It was as big as a stockyard and as charming as a prison. Thousands of us stampeded through the door. In the

---

*The Replacements were a little too smart, a certain willingness to immerse himself in cluelessness being a part of what Townshend was about. U2 seemed a little too enlightened. But, then again, it wasn't the mission of either band to be the next Who. They inspire awe on their own terms.

arena, we each stood with one foot on the seat of a folding chair and the other foot on the top of the chair in front of us, as if we were about to step up into heaven. We pointed at the stage like magnetic needles. Bottles arrived in my hands; Frisbees arced above me and sometimes toward me; pot smoke thickened the air and lightened my thoughts. The Who surged onto the stage—Keith Moon somersaulting, Daltrey lassoing the mic across the first rows of the crowd, Townshend windmilling—and ripped through a fluid, exhilarating "I Can't Explain." Then at some time, maybe during "Baba O'Riley," the green-blue lasers came on and spider-webbed through the air above the crowd, and for the only time in my life, wobbling with my feet on top of the seat of one chair and the back of another, stoned, straining upward and forward I literally reached for the light.

I might have gotten to "reached for the light" by myself. But it would have been a different experience if it were not for the critic Greil Marcus. He was the definition of a Berkeley secular humanist, and I suspect that he viewed most spiritual quests as dressed-up narcissism. But like Sister Maureen, he insisted that we were playing on a more elevated plane than we ever suspected. His rock criticism raised the stakes so high, he became my spiritual guide in spite of himself. No one I knew of had ever cared about art with this kind of passion before. His words connected the physical excitement I felt when I heard the Beatles for the first time and the sense of intellectual expansiveness I felt when Neal explained to me that we were part of an artistic tradition.

Marcus wrote the words below about the Nixon presidency, but he could have been writing about my father's death, which was just one more early seventies loss, albeit a private one:

> These are the politics of the freeze-out. They turn into a culture of seamless melancholy with the willful avoidance of anything—a book, some photographs, a record, a movie, even a newspaper—that one

suspects might produce really deep feeling. Raw emotions must be avoided when one knows they will take no shape but that of chaos.

Within such a culture there are many choices: cynicism, which is a smug, fraudulent kind of pessimism; the sort of camp sensibility that puts all feeling at a distance; or culture that reassures, counterfeits excitement and adventure, and is safe. A music as broad as rock and roll will always come up with some of each, and probably that's just as it should be.

Sometimes, though, you want something more: work so intense and compelling you will risk chaos to get close to it, music that smashes through a world that for all its desolation may be taking on too many of the comforts of familiarity.

From *Mystery Train: Images of America in Rock 'n' Roll Music*

Marcus wasn't writing about the Who. He was writing about what music could mean in a world where the charts were dominated by Olivia Newton-John ("Have You Never Been Mellow") and England Dan and John Ford Coley ("I'd Really Love to See You Tonight"). For a long time, the only flicker of the spirit in my life was music, specifically the music Pete Townshend created in the seventies.

But the Who were also exhausting—at least the way I listened to them, which was as drinking and, in moments of weakness, drugging music. Waking up after drinking too much of a quart of Yukon Jack, I would grow tired of all that damn thrashing after transcendence. You could feel the band itself grow tired. After *Quadrophenia,* they released *The Who by Numbers* and *Who Are You,* and both records felt hung over—disheveled, half wistful, half irritable, more aftermath than quest. I would grow tired of being hung over—epistemologically rattled, spiritually inelastic—although not, as it turned out, quite tired enough.

I wanted something temperate. I wanted to find my way back to the guys from the junior high lunchroom, with their jazzy ironies and healthy lives. My high school friends didn't know that they were saving me from an abyss. But when your father dies and your family evaporates, you turn to your friends. It's a hell of a burden to put on high school kids. What's even more amazing is that those guys had such rich world views, and such strong values, that they could stand up to that burden. And I wanted music that sounded like those friendships felt.

That meant Steely Dan. The guys in the lunchroom—who now included girls such as Jill Hohensee and Suzanne Gerling—loved all kinds of music ranging from jazz to ELO to Chicago, but what most of us loved best was Steely Dan. It's no wonder. For those with open ears—some people didn't like Steely Dan because they had top 40 hits and they lacked the very intemperance of the best rock—it's hard not to hear the beauty and wit in those songs. Unlike so much seventies pop, it wasn't just temperate. It didn't have the self-congratulatory taint I'd feel listening to some jazz when I would all but say to myself, "Hey, man, I'm listening to jazz," while some neo-swing bass player burbled some smug, thin solo. There was *something there* in Steely Dan, something I have never been able to express in musical terms. Although when I listened to *Pretzel Logic* drunk once, the blues underpinnings of the songs were undeniable. But those longing guitar lines in "The Boston Rag," what do you say about them?

I have been finally able to explain what I felt when I heard those songs by using the language of film. The best music of Steely Dan distills a certain kind of American movie. There is a sense of elegance, of nostalgia, of effervescence, of wisecrack, of luminosity, and of noir.

The Who promised transcendence; Steely Dan, temperance. I reached for one and then the other. But it would be years before I could experience both at the same time.

* * *

Because I had recently graduated from high school and was about to leave for Beloit College, I was especially aware of what I had come to cherish about Winona—its big trees and small houses, its sense of being cradled between the hills and the river, the homely resonances of its railroad tracks and corner bars. The June night was porous because the windows and doors were open except for screens; sprinklers *tsked* and darkened green lawns.

I stood in the living room, passing through, then loitering, and came across a show on PBS—which we rarely watched. A voice—strangely off-camera and confident, like an angel—intoned words: "Vision, timidly, becomes percussion, percussion becomes music, music becomes emotion, emotion becomes—vision." Transfixed, I watched the rest of the story, about a man taking his daughter to music lessons in a church basement.

Before I understood what this story was, I felt what it wasn't. This was not a Hemingway hero, shot and draining in a Spanish war. This was not a Fitzgerald hero, dazzled by Riverias of the soul. This was not a Faulkner hero, history-haunted and grandiloquent beneath a Coke sign. This was not a Kerouac hero, histrionic in an America so mythologized it seemed an amusement park.

This was a girl taking music lessons—in a church basement, like the ones I knew. This could have been Anita Johnson or Sue Decker or Nancy Keller. This could have been the gym at Holy Trinity of Rollingstone, where the church ladies served chicken dinners and where, on other occasions, basketballs echoed.

And, most amazingly, most liberatingly of all, "The Music School" was plotless. It was the opposite of *I Love Lucy* and every other story which held a gun to the head of what we love. It was the art of a yearning, almost spiritualized nostalgia. Circling back to read it—I ordered the book through Northern Lights, a bookstore that flickered for a few years in Winona—I discovered that it began with this surprising sentence, so unlike a conventional story opening: "My name is Alfred Schweigen and I exist in time." And its movement consisted of connections—intellectual, not actual—that the narrator made between a newspaper account of a randomly murdered acquaintance, the church's insistence that the Eucharist be chewed (not dissolved in the mouth), the narrator's own dissolving marriage, and his daughter, who is taking music lessons. Updike writes about the strange messages, accidental as litter, incisive as stars, that speak to us.

This prose is what I was looking for. It said: *existence is drama enough; the details of the world are beauty enough.*

But they weren't, quite.

* * *

I was a writer with a vocation few eighteen-year-olds had. And I'd rejected drugs, although not very well. Booze was another matter. Whiskey connected me to Hemingway and Keith Richards and Kerouac. Beer evoked being with Dad at Klinger's Bar while the golden light danced over the taps and rich shadows framed the jukebox. Alcohol let me dance with women and commune with God; it kept away the brittle chaos that seemed to threaten me while at the same time amplifying that chaos. I'd tell people that Hazelden was my safety school, but I had no intentions of giving up the booze. This would lead to complications. Jack Daniel's is, let's just say, a flawed father figure.

IV MINNEAPOLIS–ST. PAUL

APOGEE

1987. THE RINGING OF THE ALARM CLOCK STILETTOED MY sleep. My head felt dizzy and dry; nausea floated in my stomach. My cheek pressed into the burlapy fabric of something that could hardly be called a bed—the top cushion of what had been a sleeper couch. I breathed carpet deodorizer, which is little more than baking soda. The carpet deodorizer had been sprinkled on this cushion several times when, too drunk to get to the bathroom—when the space between my bed and my bathroom was a maelstrom—I'd vomited on it. Standing up made my head throb. I wanted to slump back to my couch cushion. In the shower, I leaned against the wall with one hand to steady myself. The streaming water rinsed the cigarette smoke from my hair, and as I breathed in the hot mist, my head started to clear.

Drunks are drunks, and a little of this goes a long way. Let's just say, I have never been so far away from home—however one may define home.

I was far away from the moment when I stood in our kitchen on the farm, my pajamas fluffed by the heat from the furnace, my mom bringing us cocoa and toast, my brother and sisters and Dad standing around me, their reflections in the window, reassuring me like guardian angels. I camouflaged myself in khakis and a blue oxford shirt and got on the bus, which deposited me at the advertising agency where I worked as a copywriter. I drank a lot of coffee and water and ate some packaged Danish and sometimes rested my head in my hands to get some relief.

By afternoon, every moment was a thistle. My boss wanted an ad for a library security system to feature a freckle-faced kid on a bike because, in his idyllic youth, he had watched such an ad and became forever loyal to some forgotten peanut butter. He didn't understand that I hated the soft-focus mythology of kids and picket fences. He didn't understand that I found all emotion—much less business-appropriate sentimentality—to be toxic. He didn't understand I had written poetry for years but had stopped. He didn't understand that all I wanted to do was create ads with ironic headlines and the rinsing pleasures of minimalist design. I wanted to create ads as inhuman as Spirograph orbits.

He didn't know any of this, or so I thought. Despite Lance's Ivy League degree, his stints at the leading consumer product companies, his appearances in the *Wall Street Journal,* I thought he was an idiot. He looked at me from across his desk. He resembled a certain type of British colonial official: bulldog head, thin sandy hair, a brisk moustache, and pale skin. He reddened. He brought his hands down over his face, slowly, almost painfully, like a squeegee, and then said, "I think we need to present some other options. Did you consider my idea at all?"

"Fine," I snapped, meaning, *I will* comply.

Back at my desk, the muscles in my forearm twitched and my sternum tickled. I knew that the only thing that would quiet this agitation was a drink, but I had another two hours to work.

How did I get here? How did I stray so far from home?

Yes, buried in law school for three years, I was soul-parched for the people and places I loved. I'd reached not so much a low point as a far point, an aphelion. I thirsted for the warmth I knew in Rollingstone and the wit I knew in Winona. Nostalgia ran so deep in me that it felt like grief. I longed to sit around the table at my old high school haunts—Papa John's, Bridgeman's, Westgate Bowl—or on the beach at the Pits along Highway 61 with the friends I'd made in junior high and high school after my family had dispersed. My high school friends and I always assumed that we would walk through life together and help each other along the way. It was the great shock of my early twenties to find out that was not true—not because we became disenchanted with each other but because the world naturally separated and tested us. Friends were going through their own challenges at the time: Bill Schuth and Gary Mahaffey were suffering through early divorces, others were watching career choices falter and dead end. Immersed for twelve hours a day in Contracts and Torts, lost in binge drinking with my law school classmates, isolated in a mildewy basement apartment with no phone, I had only the vaguest idea of my friends' pain.

And yes, amidst the exacting, aggressive mental life of law school, I was starving for what for me had been the true essence of education ever since I had queried Sister Maureen, had drawn my first orbits with a Spirograph, and had written game summaries in my Viking Book: the pursuit of meaning and making. And yes, I was afraid of entering the work world—and unsure if I was suited to law. And, yes, I was at a time in my life when an almost instinctual need to find someone to share my life with surged under everything else I did.

That needy self—lost, jealous, volatile, determined to dig its own abyss—had completely screwed up a romantic relationship, and when one night in May 1984, with the sirens of *Hill Street Blues* in the background, the woman in question said, "Enough," I marched to a bar on Central Avenue and drank three Special Exports and punctuated them with three shots of Jim Beam in ten minutes. Although the quantities themselves were not that scary, I knew what I felt as I ordered those drinks: *I will need to drink every day for the rest of my life.*

*

Day after day, I traveled from work downtown to my apartment to my favorite bars, a distance shorter than the distance from the farm to the village in Rollingstone. Eventually the rest of the world fell away. That included my family. The lure of Petula Clark's "Downtown" had brought Sheila to Minneapolis, where she worked as a nurse, but I rarely saw her. Colleen and Tom thrived on the abandoned farmstead they had bought outside of Winona. A stream flowed through their place and pooled into a duck pond. They raised ducks and turkeys and rabbits. I saw them and their three children on holidays. Maureen and Lowell lived in Colorado with their four boys. Dennis and Doris lived in Washington with their extended family. They were pushpins on a map, not family. I talked to Mom on the phone once a week, editing my life down to ten acceptable minutes, and she reduced the rest of the family to a synopsis.

Picking me up for a Christmas drive to Winona, Sheila arrived at a post–law school apartment I shared with some guys I barely knew, saw the bottles and cigarettes and other aftermaths of partying (for a change, not mine), and wept. When I lost a job due to hung-over insubordination, I couldn't bear to tell Mom, so I called Colleen, drunk, every night for several weeks from a pay phone. But I was largely absent, and I now believe absence is a sin because it rehearses the greater absence of death. I didn't know then but I know now what it feels like to have calls go unreturned.

So on that day in 1987 or thereabouts, on that day when I had woken hung over and ashamed, the bar thrived in my mind as I left work—its neon signs smiled, the windows liquefied sunlight, its varnished wood reassured me, its shadowy interiors welcomed me, its pool tables glowed. And it was not lost on me, even at the time, that I had loved bars since those rides to the creamery and Klinger's with Dad when I was a toddler. I was not simply an alcoholic. I was a bar person. I sought peace in places.

*

Around me, the actual world—a crowded bus crossing the Hennepin Bridge—sputtered like a hive. So when I disembarked and crossed University Avenue to Sports Central, a bar a few blocks from my apartment, I walked with the contained fervor of a swimmer walking toward a lake. The place was crowded, and I knew many of the people here. I nodded to them, but I sought the bartender, Linda. I inhaled, but probably didn't notice, the place's malty, muddy smell. Linda caught my eye to confirm my regular order, then brought me a Special Export. I drank it. In Special Export, the alcohol is a sharp presence. I put a twenty on the bar, which Linda harvested as I drank succeeding beers.

I looked around. When I had first come in there alone, I knew no one, but I slowly accumulated friends. Next to me might be Rod, a divorced medical technician who earned a Silver Star in Vietnam, or my neighbor Tom Rock, a big, sarcastic, smiling American Indian who worked as a forklift operator. Like Rod, he found his way to the cheap apartments in this neighborhood when he divorced. At Halloween, he missed the trick-or-treaters of his former life so much that he once leaned out of the second-story window of his security building apartment and threw wrapped candies at passing children. The children giggled; their mothers whisked them away.

Or I might see Curt, who could be cast as Robert Bly (white-haired, with a face both fleshy and hawkish) but with a more picaresque résumé—computer programmer, accountant for a small city, janitor. When I got a ride home from Curt one night, paperbacks swarmed the backseat of his car like bats in a cave. He once owned a used bookstore and couldn't bear to give away the last of his inventory. I drank with men who had lost their marriages and their businesses.

If the phone rang and Linda was busy with a customer, Curt would answer the phone, "Sports Central, maître d'." If I got him talking, Curt would tell me to read Joseph Mitchell and Peter De Vries. He would tell me about when Hubert Humphrey was mayor, when the city was menaced by Jewish and Swedish gangs, when the Minneapolis Millers played. But Curt would also blush when someone new to the bar said, "Curt, you still hanging out on Lake Street?" He had never mentioned his Lake Street adventures in Sports Central. While Sports Central was unfashionable but benign—slumming college students would yell "Norm!" when they came in—Lake Street was a far more dangerous place, a place where you might stumble into a drug deal or fencing operation. Those of us who were regulars at Sports Central had secret lives that bumped into secret lives, a wardrobe of lives.

Curt was me in two decades. We called ourselves *bar people*, and we knew that, in nine cases out of ten, the term euphemized addiction, but we also knew we loved something besides alcohol—a gregariousness, or at least the accoutrements of gregariousness. We were pack animals who had been cut off from our packs. Whatever else it was, this place was the opposite of an empty apartment.

The twenty was depleted. The happy hour rush had subsided. My mind was glossy and glad. I decided to venture somewhere else because things now seemed possible. My tolerance for alcohol was so high that, eight beers into the night, I didn't stagger, but I wouldn't have minded dancing. And I was hungry. I ventured to Nye's or maybe Arone's, where I knew the bartenders and where I could order something to eat. I lived on bar food: Tombstone pizzas, burgers and fries. And there might be women there. I felt too bloated with drinking, too twitchy and alienated, too damaged and ashamed, to pursue any women sober, but the women who showed up then, after happy hour, were themselves a little lost—a single mom suffering in a suburban insurance office who every so often left her kid with a sitter and went out by herself, a woman who had just moved there and who visited bars while her boyfriend worked in Washington and who mumbled to herself, "Maybe this time it will be different."

But often there was no one, and I chatted with my friends the bartenders: Chet, a soft-spoken man who had worked at Nye's since he was a bus boy in high school and who was now in his fifties; Denny at Arone's, a burly, friendly former garbage man who always shook my hand ceremoniously. Bartenders liked me. I drank a lot but didn't pick fights or get loud. I chatted, sometimes obsessively, but they knew how to handle that. I tipped big. A conversation with a bartender is a commercial transaction, but these men—decent, deft—did not emphasize this.

Ten elided to eleven. I headed back toward home but stopped at Sports Central for a face new or familiar—my mind, liquid; my steps, erratic; moving to the soundtrack of beers swishing through my consciousness. Maybe I talked with Linda in the emptying bar, her face sharp and quick smiling. She was an orphan, twenty-three years in the Twin Cities, three at the U, twenty working in bars like this, her own husband a different kind of drunk, a stay-at-home drunk, a dimming lamp of a human being.

Or maybe I talked with Curt's brother, Cal. Cal was a white-haired architect with the walking-into-the-wind face of George Washington. He was also a Stalinist who maintained, despite the purges, that the great man had done what was necessary to "drag Russia kicking and screaming into the twentieth century." But what baffled me most about Cal wasn't his politics but his decades-long marriage. How did he insinuate his daily drinking into his marriage? I was terrified that any woman I might love would discover how I lived and be done with me. I didn't ask him about this, for obvious reasons. Cal and I talked sports. The Stalinist had been a pretty good softball pitcher.

Eleven o'clock fumbled into midnight. I was without self-control, but I wasn't without self-knowledge. I was not offering up any hard truths on my own, but if you had said to me, "These bars are filled with men who are the age your father was when he died, and that's not a coincidence," I would have agreed. For years I'd been trying to piece together a patchwork father, an abstraction of values made of friends and art and mentors and memories and distant good men, but I still craved the real thing—a guy I could talk politics and sports with, a guy I could smoke cigars and play poker with.

Stumbling home, I got down my copy of John Cheever's *Collected Stories* and crawled onto the raft of a favorite paragraph:

> These stories seem at times to be stories of a long-lost world when the city of New York was still filled with a river light, when you heard the Benny Goodman quartets from a radio in the corner stationery store, and when almost everybody wore a hat. Here is the last of that generation of chain smokers who woke the world in the morning with their coughing, who used to get stoned at cocktail parties and perform obsolete dance steps like "the Cleveland Chicken," sail for Europe on ships, who were truly nostalgic for love and happiness, and whose gods were as ancient as yours and mine, whoever you are.

And I thought of my father, who never traveled east of Indiana, never lived in a city, and never boarded a ship. And I thought pitifully of his salmon socks, his lime ties, his Hai Karate splashes, his Dutch Masters cigars, his love of bars and his love of dancing, and his penchant for singing "May the Bird of Paradise Fly Up Your Nose," the goofiness of a hip bone that became a stick shift. I thought of his high school yearbook. The class had predicted what each member would be. In 1938, in prairie-locked Illinois, his friends looked at Maurice Fenton and saw an ocean liner captain.

During the day, I trafficked in ironies and minimalisms. I hated emotion. The only sentimental ads I created were the ones in my head, the private ones for my past, in those moments before I passed out.

* * *

Alcoholism couldn't bleach the days entirely. I held a color separation: 11" x 17" film of a spread of a brochure for a 3M product used for creating the templates for circuit boards. Ric Peltier, the art director I worked with, had presented it to me as a courtesy but also because, like me, he enjoyed that moment when the long process of meetings and thinking and revision had precipitated something we could hold in our hands. When I held the acetate, four layers of film shifted beneath my fingers, misaligning slightly, blurring the image with out-of-registration rainbows. I knew what would happen when I lifted the layers, so the moment offered the pleasure of a magic trick repeated. Each layer contained the exact image of the pages, reduced to one color: magenta, cyan, yellow, and black. Each was a Warhol. This was how color printing worked—through an algebra of color, all images resolved into their component red, blue, and yellow, with black added for crispness. This was how *Wonders of the Animal Kingdom* was born. When I let the sheets of film fall back together again, all colors blossomed.

I did not get to this moment—holding this crisp, colored acetate that glimmered like a stream in the sun—directly. Life tugged and hinted and nudged, often without my comprehension and contrary to my plans. My senior year in college, I had spent fall semester studying with twenty other students in the Newberry Library in Chicago. Chicago frightened me. The El, a machine the size of a city, rumbled. Blocks of anonymous buildings stretched for miles. I felt claustrophobic standing outside. The possibility of crime simmered in the air. Standing on a bus, my hands grabbing an overhead bar to steady myself, distracted by a stranger's question about a satchel I carried, I was pickpocketed. I felt more fooled than violated. When I entered the window-grated pawnshop to buy a new wallet, the clerk's expression radiated a particular kind of condescension: *I live in this world. You have to enter it now, soft small-town boy. Don't think that makes you better.*

A staff member at the Newberry Library also sang with the Lyric Opera of Chicago, and he asked me and two of my seminar-mates to serve as waiters at a Christmas party he was having. He lived in a beautiful brick townhouse in West Chicago, one of the first gentrified neighborhoods. He sent us two blocks to get some supplies at a store that had signs in Spanish. When we left the store, a squad car stopped, and two officers emerged and pointed their guns at shadows across the street. Startled, my friends and I scurried back to the party. Our anecdote fizzed inside us. We became proud of our ability to walk through cities.

Scary Chicago affirmed my post-graduation plans: I would attend the University of Minnesota Law School, and I would set up a practice in Winona. There, I would be in a position to be close to Rollingstone and to be a part of lives, and I would write the stories and poems of Winona. I would fulfill the ambition that first formed in my teenage heart when I fused the examples of Leo Murphy and William Faulkner.

But I was amazed at how quickly I had transformed the emerging cops and drawn guns into a story and at how the incident made the rest of the night effervesce and how what I remembered was the food—Italian sausage sandwiches—and the Lyric Opera singers belting out Christmas carols and, as we left the party, the glowing embers of the lights of the townhouse in the city.

Chicago germinated something in me—a love of cities that was not quite ready to ripen. The second half of the semester I spent there was devoted to writing a hundred-page research paper, which allowed me to take some afternoons off and ride the bus to the Art Institute. There, I would stand in front of the bright, disobedient art in the white rooms. My seminar-mates and I ate the city's abundant gyros and Italian beef sandwiches and attended vintage movies and sought out music—the Iron City Houserockers surging in a second-floor club that looked like Philip Marlowe's office, Tom Waits swaying and quipping in a cocktail lounge, the Kinks vamping in a Northside theater. We played touch football and ultimate Frisbee in the strips of green by the lake. Beyond that green were the Gold Coast condominiums where Bob Newhart returned to Emily.

We all came from small colleges in academic towns, and before that we came from small towns or suburbs—Northfield, Minnesota; Houghton, Michigan; Ames, Iowa; Chevy Chase, Maryland; Edina, Minnesota; Decatur, Georgia; and Fenton, Michigan. We came to study the proposition "Public v. Private: The Dilemma of Liberalism: 1660–1960." But what we really sought was Chicago. The liberalism we studied wasn't what's meant by liberalism today. It was not the platform of the Democratic Party—although that was one historical outgrowth of this thinking—but classical liberalism, free markets and unleashed expression and liberated polities, the platform of Adam Smith and James Madison, an opposition to feudalism and mercantilism. It was precisely those liberating forces that swirled in this city and manifested themselves in high-rise condominiums and Spanish convenience stores and drawn guns. My friends and I were both liberalism's products and its students, propelled there by the wise accidents and half-understood attractions of a kind of spiritual free market. But, as in the case of much of my life, I wouldn't realize the effect that Chicago had on me until much later.

According to plan, I went to law school. I studied the kind of general law that might be useful in a town like Winona. I took the agricultural law class mentioned earlier. I found that I quite enjoyed the academic study of law, but, from what I could glimpse, the practice of law was a relentless race between language and contingency. What if this happened? What if this happened? What if this happened? It rewarded prolific, precise, analytically agile minds, and, although I was doing well enough in law school, those were not my strengths. I feared I would forget a key piece of language and a client's farm would be lost. I couldn't face that.

And I realized that Chicago had vaccinated me—I didn't fear cities anymore. As I walked the streets near the law school, I started seeing these bus stop posters: A picture of Richard Nixon and the headline *You can't cover up a bad haircut. 7th South 8th for Hair.* A picture of a goalie's face overprinted with the headline *Snap. Crackle. Pop. Without the milk and sugar. Minnesota North Stars Hockey.* A piece of art from the Minneapolis Art Institute's exhibition of 1930s abstraction: *After four years of Herbert*

Hoover, you'd reject reality, too. These ads rewarded cleverness; their buoyant advocacy was the opposite of law. And they were *designed*—headlines detonated the energy in visuals; their clean, kerned typography was a kind of super fluency. They flowed and clicked from image to headline to logo like machines. This—not law—was what I wanted to do.

And so in 1987, at the agency, on a night when we've worked late, my friends Ric and Mike and I stand at opposite corners of a large open area in our old brick office building. The clubs of Minneapolis's warehouse district are five stories below us. The windows reflect the lights of our office back at us. Pushpins secure award-winning ads—*this is what I want to do*—and our magic-markered layouts—*this is what I could do*—to burlap-textured cube walls. Mike, who works as a keyliner (a now antique job), has collected hundreds of bits of tape into a ball larger than a softball but still graspable. We stand as far away from each other as possible and play catch. The ball is so big that it is planetary. It wobbles on my hand. As I accelerate it forward, I can feel its mass become momentum. Ric or Mike catches it and flings it back at me. The recreational fear of a roller coaster ride tickles me as the tape ball approaches; the dissipation of fear elates me when I catch it. These are boys' pleasures: the pleasures of *whipping*, as a verb meaning to throw recklessly. Any women in the office cover their heads with their hands and flee. We all can go home now, but we don't want to. For the twenty minutes we toss the ball, I'm so happy, I don't even want to drink.

OF ALL MY WINONA FRIENDS, Bill Schuth's brother Joe reminds me most of my dad. Once, when I stumbled home from a bar to an empty apartment and stood at my answering machine—melodramatic, swaying, stupid with alcohol—I discovered that Joe, then a graphic designer in Minneapolis, had left me a message that said, "If you're around, you've gotta watch Bewitched *on Nick at Nite; it's the one where Darrin's having a kid."*

A few months later, another drunk, another message from a bright voice in a suburban home: "Are you watching Freddie and the Dreamers on The Best of Ed Sullivan? *They're doing this dance called the Freddie, and it just might be the most Caucasian thing I've ever seen." It's as if the guys who sat around the table together in junior high and high school were sending a representative to save me.*

THE PATH BACK HOME—
AND SISTER MAUREEN'S RECIPE FOR GOD

I HAD LITERATURE THAT I READ LIKE PRAYERS WHEN I was hung over. I could understand only some Geoffrey Hill, but I held onto these lines from his poem "Funeral Music," addressed to the martyred Muslim intellectual Averroes. I used them as both balm and reprimand when a hangover pulsed through my brain:

> Averroes, old heathen,
> If only you had been right, if Intellect
> Itself were absolute law, sufficient grace,
> Our lives would be a myth of captivity
> Which we might enter: an unpeopled region
> Of ever new-fallen snow, a palace blazing
> With perpetual silence, as with torches.

On one or two Saturday mornings, when I had managed not to drink the night before, when my head was clear for a few hours, and breathing refreshed my lungs rather than nauseating me, and the warming spring sunlight filtered through the leaves of the elm trees in the park near my apartment, I would think of the opening of John Updike's story "Leaves":

> The grape leaves outside my window are curiously beautiful. "Curiously" because it comes upon me as strange, after the long darkness of self-absorption and fear and shame in which I have been living, that things are beautiful, that independent of our catastrophes they continue to maintain the casual precision, the effortless abundance of inventive "effect," which is the hallmark and specialty of nature. Nature: this morning it seems very clear to me that Nature may be defined as that which exists without guilt. Our bodies are in nature; our shoes, their laces, the little plastic tips of the laces—everything around us and about us is in Nature, and yet something holds us away from it, like the upward push of water which keeps us from touching the sandy bottom, ribbed and glimmering with crescental fragments of oyster shell, so clear to our eyes.

The details in this passage—the little plastic tips of shoelaces, the crescental fragments of oyster shells—reassured like the *Wonders of the Animal Kingdom.* These long Latinate phrases soothed like the Mass. Compare "they continue to maintain the casual precision, the effortless abundance of inventive 'effect,' which is the hallmark and specialty of nature" with "from east to west he gathers a people to himself so that from east to west a perfect offering may be made."

I had been carrying bits of John Updike stories with me since the summer after high school, a few years after my meeting with Neal at Papa John's, at a time when I had grown tired of things happening.

The Updike who wrote these stories was kin to my Winona friends who sat around lunch tables and quoted Bob Newhart and who sang entire Steely Dan albums while they ran cross-country. Both Updike's early stories and Steely Dan albums promised a relief from the punishments of rebellion; a relief from the full disclosure of drunken vomiting and penitence of hangovers, which felt in their dryness, their insistence, their judgment, their incensey fluttering in the capillaries and hands, and their association with guilt, like Latin; and from underachieving mediocrity at high school; and from the instant abysses of pot. They both promised that you might wake up on a Saturday with a clear head and a clear self, able to appreciate the subtleties of the world.

But these sentences were not enough: they somehow lacked spiritual stamina. It's probably no accident that while he could write radiant short stories, Updike the novelist was jaded and narcissistic. He was a wonderful son but a horrible father. His autobiography barely mentions his children.

I was spiritually sick, and, like most epiphanies, Updike's beautiful sentences weren't weight bearing.

There was something wrong with me, that twitching in my forearms and the clenching in my sternum, which could be soothed only with a drink. The more I needed that drink, the better bars looked in my mind. My mind shined the glasses hanging above the bar and mopped the muddy floor. Sports Central was once again a place of camaraderie with men and, on a good day, possibility with women. And by noon, I would walk into a beckoning bar, and the cycle would begin again.

Updike himself knew that the stories in which I sought refuge were not enough. He ended "The Music School" with these lines: "The world is the host. It must be chewed." I refused to chew the dry, difficult world. I needed to find a spiritual engine for my life—an engine as vigorous as my alcoholism.

* * *

"*. . . who used to get stoned at cocktail parties and perform obsolete dance steps like 'the Cleveland Chicken,' sail for Europe on ships . . .*" I hold this romantic picture of a man brightened by a few beers, but my father drank more like I did than I remember. I also have always pictured Dennis's boyhood as idyllic. He spent summer days with Father, who taught him how to farm. He was driving tractors by twelve. It wasn't that simple.

Dennis recently told me that Dad—who, unlike Cheever's heroes, had no cruise ships to escape to—would sometimes disappear for hours on his personal ocean. Dennis remembers being nine and knowing that Saturday was the day for cleaning the barn but also watching Dad leave in the morning with a friend of his. So Dennis got the cows out of the barn, swept the shit and urine-spattered straw into the gutters and pitchforked it out of the building, mopped the floors, pulled bales of straw out of the loft and distributed the clean straw, and then rebedded all twenty-plus cows. That morning in Washington State, Dennis said, "You don't think of it as anything strange. You think, 'This will make it easier for Dad.'"

When Dad returned home, all he had to do was the milking. If Dad drank like me, he was serene, not angry, and his drunkenness showed up only as a pervasive smell of beer, a tendency to talk too much, an eagerness to dance, and an occasional befuddled accident—a dropped milk can, a slip. But no drunk is wholly benign, especially when he is a father and husband. On one of my rare trips to Winona in those years, Mom told me that the only thing that might have broken them up was "your father's drinking when we were first married." Caught up in my own problems, I didn't make much of that statement at the time.

I make much of it now, perhaps too much. I have thought of fatherlessness as my cross to bear, but Dennis's may have been even heavier: he had to *be* Dad when Dad wasn't up to it.

And I was free to absorb lesson after lesson about what it meant it to be a responsible man from Dennis and Mom and then a series of remarkable friends. I could look to the enthusiasm of Neal, the diligence of Gary, the rectitude and curiosity of my more clean-cut friends such as Bill Schuth and Chris Baudhuin. At Beloit, Tom McBride taught me that the English language, properly used, was a tool for accomplishing important work. At the Newberry program, a number of public-spirited friends, especially Dave Schultz, thought with the seriousness and subtlety of the best constitutional scholars and lived with the bravery of the best prosecutors. They worried the same questions that bothered the Founders. In my sober thirties, Steve Seefeldt showed me that one did not have to give up one's bluesy dark side to be a decent guy, and my wife, Ellen, has helped me discover, through years of insightful conversation, how one can be effective and empathetic in the world. And those are just a few of the friends who've helped me become me.

It is amazing how many role models I had, if I had just bothered to look and act. In high school, I made an alcoholic's mistake, conflating resentment with rebellion, so I didn't notice that I *never took action* on the various judgments and fervors in my head. I was semiferal, with a brittle arrogance and robust selfishness, and thus clueless. But not entirely clueless: I watched as my friends Celia Henderson and Molly Murphy and Mike Russell actually lobbied for better teachers when it became clear that many of our social studies teachers were coaches first and teachers second. I still use the lessons suggested by these small acts of bravery—be impeccable so you can be credible; be charming and well-mannered and specific in your requests—as touchstones for leading a grown-up life. These students were liberals, and when I think of them, I conclude that liberal guilt is in most cases a myth. They embodied a politics that might better be called liberal gratefulness, although I've seen enough gracious conservatives and spiteful liberals to think the content of one's politics is almost coincidental. What one thinks of the roles of government and business, the strictness or flexibility of constitutional interpretation, and the proper expenditures for national defense are ultimately empirical and tactical matters. The political question that matters to me is, are you grateful? Or are you resentful? Are you generous? Or are you tribal? Are you willing to look at facts? Have you avoided the hard work of policy by gussying up some favorite clichés as principles? Here was the gift within the loss: because I lost a father, I looked for a father and, in the process, found some remarkable friends.

* * *

1991. February in Minnesota. Winter distends into grey skies and soiled snow, the self distends into sadness, and, home for the weekend, I sit at what had been Klinger's Bar in Rollingstone. The roads have changed since my boyhood. Highway 248 no longer passes through Rollingstone but sweeps, unimpeded, around it, with a turnoff for Rollingstone. But this raises the question, unimpeded to what? There are no larger towns on its path. Some miles up the ridge, it reaches Highway 31, which leads to the town of Altura, population 417, and beyond that a state park. Highway planners cannot be sentimental, but this rerouting goes beyond realistic to being mean. There is among the administrative class—the people who plan bus schedules and reroute highways—a contempt for small towns. They are inefficient. True enough, it's a judgment made by people who refuse to weigh the inefficiency of small towns—their drain on school district budgets, their slowing of traffic to ostensibly more important places—against their value, the way they create pockets of meaning and happiness.

I'm alternating beers and nonalcoholic beers so I can drive, sitting at a bar more scuffed and a floor more dirty—like the floor of a shed, not a house—than I remembered. I've explained what I do to the guy sitting next to me. He said, "So you're basically a glorified salesman." In a sense, I agreed with him. Advertising was first defined as *salesmanship in print,* and a senior copywriter at Fallon McElligott, the agency that created the ads that nudged me into the business, described himself to me as an "introverted salesman." But *glorified* is a machete of a word; I'm being cut down to size.

I get in my car and drive back toward Winona. Both hung over and drunk, unsure of my reflexes, my eyes digesting dismal February, the off-white fields and five o'clock shadow of leafless trees on the hills, I wait cautiously at the stop. But finally I pull onto the highway and pass the Literskis'.

Like Rollingstone, Minnesota City has been bypassed; in this case, Highway 61 sweeps around it. The towns I grew up in have become limbs without blood. I turn onto a highway that has been demoted to a frontage road and stop at the L-Cove, a roadhouse just before town. I want only real beers now. I sit at the bar and drink, and I feel as lucky as a man sitting by a river.

A couple of beers into this, someone I know comes in—someone I'd been in a couple of classes with in junior high, someone who knows people I know, someone whose mom I worked with one summer at a dry cleaners. He is accompanied by people I don't know. He is pleasant and tactful and comes over and says "hi," asks what I'm doing. I tell him that I'm in advertising. He rejoins his friends, who talk about concerts they have seen in the Cities. I ask the bartender to call a cab. I drink alone at the bar with nothing left to say to the bartender, too aware of the chiming conversation behind me. My cab takes ten minutes to arrive. They tick by.

When I arrive at the Winona apartment where my mom has retired, I read in the paper that my friend Gary's dad died this weekend—in his early fifties, his warmhearted life shortened and saddened by drinking. I am so drunk I don't want to go anywhere, but I call Gary and express my condolences. I watch TV with Mom, who tells me I am wise to not drive drunk. Otherwise, she treats me as if I have a cold whose symptoms include wobbling and ranting. The room is too hot. I am surrounded by the wall hangings and knickknacks Mom has accumulated over the course of sixty years. There is a painted plate that my father had liked; its green script reads, "May you be in heaven a half an hour before the devil knows you're dead." I fall asleep on the couch.

The next morning, I take a cab back out to Minnesota City to get my car. When I return to St. Paul—I have moved from Minneapolis—I write a single, shame-soaked, thousand-word paragraph in my journal. It is the only journal entry I have ever destroyed. Two weeks later, I will quit drinking, presumably for good.

On that road between Rollingstone and Minnesota City, on that February weekend, I had intersected my history. When I spoke to my brother in Washington State, he said that, when he was fifteen, he and Dad were in the pickup, driving between Minnesota City and Rollingstone, and, about halfway between the Literskis' and the Kendricks', Dad—who had taken too many pain pills—was weaving over the center line. When the cops pulled the truck over, Dennis explained that Dad was on prescription painkillers. When the cop asked if Dennis could drive, he said, "Yes, I have a farm license," and he got Dad home.

Is this overwhelming sense of responsibility and powerlessness what pushed Dennis into the Marines and then Vietnam? I don't know. But Dennis told me that in Vietnam, he had taken a liberal amount of LSD. He did this even though a friend of his had overdosed and, his mind broken, had been admitted to whatever psych wards existed in Vietnam in the 1960s. As the drug took effect, Dennis felt his mind leaving his body, and he gasped at his future, sedated and babbling in asylums. He prayed, "God, if you give me my mind back, I will serve you the rest of my life." And Dennis kept that promise, carrying his religion lightly but vigorously, agreeing to full-body baptism in a church dunking tank, not being afraid to preach in the streets among homeless teens, not being afraid to invite drug addicts into his beautiful home if he thought it would help them.

I do know that I was set to carry forward the worst of my father's legacy: his resentment, his sense of being an outsider, his sense of never feeling at home in that place that I had always thought of as our family's Eden. My life could have been a sour, childless, solitary version of my father's.

A week sober, I stood in the bathroom of the apartment I shared with my Winona friend Daryl Lanz. Since quitting, I had had trouble sleeping. My sternum still twitched. My arms still felt hollow. I was throwing my blankets off. I breathed—consciously, deeply—and said, "God grant me the serenity to accept the things I cannot change, the courage to change the things I can, and the wisdom to know the difference," but it was really only the first phrase I cared about. I surrendered to a God I could not define but whose power I could not deny because it had moved through my limbs and stopped their twitching, and moved through my sternum and quieted its spasms, and moved through my mind and eased the internal combustion of its resentments. I had surrendered, I had confessed, I had sat in rooms that smelled of cheap coffee and cigarettes with people who had done the same, and I felt the divine for the first time in my life. I knew for the first time what Sister Maureen meant when she repeated Christ's words, "Wherever two or more of you are gathered in my name, there I shall be." And I knew that Sister Maureen's promise was true even when the name of Christ was not invoked. I repeated the prayer until it became a mantra, until it was a word that became a self, until I was as calm as the purple dusk outside my window. This took a while. I will never elegantly accept the world. But I had come to the end of what my first-draft mind and terrier willpower could accomplish.

The months after I quit drinking were staticky and sludgy. At a lunch at Café di Napoli in downtown Minneapolis, a law school friend of mine joked, "Standards are so low today. You show up for work. You pay your bills. You're a saint!" I laughed with him.

Around this time, the school district threatened to close the Rollingstone Elementary School. I've moved too often, so I wasn't contacted when a group of alums organized to save the school. I didn't follow up when I overheard someone mention the fundraising efforts. Other alums, working with State Representative Gene Pelowski, raised $100,000 and saved the elementary school while I congratulated myself for showing up for work and paying my bills.

MY FAVORITE MOVIE FROM those years was Diner, *in which high school friends who've stumbled into the world—into marriages and graduate school and increasingly desperate drinking—keep circling back to a favorite diner because they cannot bear the possibility of becoming unmoored from their pasts. It brings me back to times in college, home for the holidays, standing with my friends, at two in the morning, in the brisk air outside some all-night joint, before everybody finally calls it a night: this feels like home. Someone has flirted futilely with the waitress, but it's a stag moment. (Women don't much like* Diner *and for good reason—the women in it are complications or burdens or objectives or simply reminders of one's cluelessness. "What fucking Chisholm Trail?" indeed.)*

One of the guys has probably said at least one funny thing we will always remember. If someone does something stupid, it will become a story, not a complication. The objects nearby—the chrome napkin holders, the cigarette smoke, the ketchup bottles, the radiant jukebox—feel sacramental: the outward manifestations of inward grace.

A HEART-SIZED ROLLINGSTONE

I AM NOSTALGIC. I WROTE THIS MEMOIR BECAUSE I HAVE a crush on the past. I love the game Twister; streamlined toasters and ottomans with atomic/cocktail motifs;. TV shows such as *Laugh-In, The Avengers, Get Smart,* and *Batman;* the originals of the movies *Charade* and *Ocean's 11;* and the music of Dave Brubeck and Stan Getz. A part of me thinks the world of my youth was kinder and richer than the world I live in now. It took me a long time to realize that the part of me that romanticizes the past could become toxic.

At lunch in 1995, a friend recommends a book, David Gelernter's *Drawing Life.* Gelernter, a computer scientist at Yale, wrote *Drawing Life* when he was recovering from injuries suffered when he opened a package from the Unabomber.

Those injuries were awful. Shocked when his mail attacked him, Gelernter wandered the Yale campus, bleeding. He would spend weeks on his back in hospital beds. He would undergo painful therapies and frightening surgeries. He would be raked by pain and dulled by drugs. His dreams tortured him. He could not see out of one eye. An author and artist, he couldn't use his right hand to write or paint, and he could barely type. For months, he could not do anything that required two hands—take a casserole out of the oven, drive. At the end of the book, he was still unable to play catch with his sons. And these physical injuries inevitably led to psychological anguish—a condition Gelernter called, with noble accuracy, discouragement.

When I think of Gelernter, I think of my dad when I stole his cane and he was trapped on the bed. They were both literal victims of actual accidents. For both of them, the battle against the strange mix of inertia and venom that can pool in our minds when we aren't working was particularly challenging. I need to cut my dad a little slack.

Despite injuries that would give other men an excuse to stay home and collect disability, despite a setback that I fear would have tipped me into drink or gluttony, Gelernter persevered. He returned to class and taught. He gained back some vision and some use of his right hand. He learned to drive. He wrote not one but two books.

In some ways, Gelernter was sympathetic to me even before the bombing. He would have felt right at home at that junior high lunch table with Bill Schuth and Pat Marcotte and Steve Collins and Jim Marley and the rest of the guys. We would have welcomed his enthusiasm for the charm of black and white movies and the optimism of the 1939 World's Fair, for the more inspiring parts of history and the more aesthetically pleasing aspects of science, for the dense and detailed reporting of Joseph Mitchell and the celebratory paintings of Stuart Davis. I'm fascinated with Gelernter because, although he's never lived west of upstate New York, he seems a representative Winona guy.

And, yet, by the end of Gelernter's book, I simply didn't want to spend any more time with this man.

As with me, Gelernter's happy place is an era he didn't actually live through: the first half of the twentieth century. He makes lingering stops in turn-of-the-century children's magazines (he loves the kids' earnest poetry) and the 1939 World's Fair. Gelernter claims that his immersion in the pop culture of the first half of the century is therapy, a "soothing refuge"—and who can begrudge him that? In fact, it's an absolute joy to be reminded of those inspiring couplets written by children, those saucy Ginger Rogers retorts, those elegant Fred Astaire dances, and the streamlined trains and diners of the World's Fair.

You also can't begrudge Gelernter his rage. He wants the Unabomber executed not for what he did to him but what he could have done to his family. He understands that criminals don't just harm us physically but that they also poison the air we breathe by infusing it with fear. He has no time for the Unabomber's "theories" and no sympathy for the insanity defense, and he despises the press's amoral fascination with the man.

But the book starts to go bad early on, when he asserts that in 1996, "terrorism has become a part of life" in ways it never was before, that "crime has gotten so much worse," that "street crime was practically non-existent in New York in 1936," and that "this long ago society bristled with contempt" for criminals.

I recognized this world view immediately. The present always strikes me as a corrupted, volatile version of a happier, saner past. I think of my own childhood as a Disney movie in which Gerald Ford and Hubert Humphrey make sensible compromises. This simply isn't true. My actual childhood was punctuated by news of assassinations, bombings, riots, and lynchings.

Gelernter is similarly deluded. People a hundred years ago were every bit as familiar with terrorism as people in 1996. An anarchist killed President McKinley. In 1919, other anarchists mailed thirty bombs in one day and then, a few months later, simultaneously set off bombs in eight American cities. In the 1930s, John Dillinger was worshipped as a folk hero in ways that the Unabomber never was. Homicide levels in the 1930s were about the same as 1990s homicides, with highs around ten incidents per 100,000 people and lows around six per 100,000.

Gelernter acknowledges his sloppiness about the basic facts justifying his critique and doesn't care. He claims that *Drawing Life* is a serious cultural critique, an urgent attempt to "come to grips with basic questions about Modern America." At the same time, he notes that "the theorizing was done under stress and the niceties were not observed." Of course, he never considers the possibility that intellectual and moral negligence rationalized as passion—i.e., his book—might be precisely what's wrong with Modern America. Gelernter doesn't limit his contempt to his attacker: "At the 1996 convention, Republicans lavished attention on AIDS victims and rape victims, former welfare mothers and powerful female politicians, god *bless 'em everyone . . .* " [italics his].

Gelernter's writing isn't bad because it ends in anger. Much good writing ends in anger. It's bad writing because it starts in hatred. It's bad writing because he confuses pathology with philosophy. It's bad writing because he makes positions you agree with—the Unabomber's ideas deserve no serious attention; the press can be boorish; stay-at-home moms deserve respect; emptying prisons is irresponsible; experience should inform abstract ideas—seem repellent. He too often sacrifices moral precision for moral clarity because moral clarity allows him the satisfactions of rage.

One of the pillars of the traditional America Gelernter rhapsodizes about is prayer. Yet in a personal book about recovery from a horrible, unjust accident, he never privately prays. I wish he had. It might have eased his pain and alleviated the hatred that twists his prose and his logic.

Gelernter's book is toxic because he lost (at least temporarily) one of the essential adult battles—the battle against your own neuroses, your own resentments, your own rage (my personal nemesis), your own despair, your own intellectual limitations and delusions, your own private entropies and inertias, your own tendency to become a pool of rancid opinions on a couch. These are not just character defects. They are character viruses.

They attack us. Even without the help of a bomb in your mail, they paste you to the couch, narrow your life, and twist your thinking, especially your politics, until it becomes increasingly more virulent and less vigorous. And those character viruses feed on self-righteousness. Self-righteousness is the most powerful vice because it feels so much like a virtue.

Nostalgia is a sidekick of self-righteousness. Nostalgia is *inherently* delusional—which makes it good entertainment but horrible history. It condemns the present and sugarcoats the past. When Winona guys go bad—when they sink into despair, when they drop out, when they become angry and alienated—they take the same route Gelernter took.

Reading *Drawing Life*'s angry sentimentality, I realized that I had spent too much time stagnating on barstools, seduced by my own past, pissed off at the real present. I realized there was something almost natal about my love for boomerang shapes on highball glasses and Brubeck tunes. These happy, dangling trapezoids were a mobile in a crib.

At some point, you need to grow up. Memories need to become values, and values need to become actions, or they go bad. At some point, you need to forgive the present for not being the past. At some point, you need to stop keening after your romanticized old culture and pitch in with the rest of the flawed humans and build a new one.

* * *

And yet nostalgia has persisted for me, long past the first drafts of this book, and it can play a positive role as well.

I am now fifty-three, and I may have prostate cancer. If you're going to have cancer, it's the one you'd want. That said, nothing reminds you of your mortality like a biopsy. You're barely covered by one of those little gowns. You're numbed but conscious. Needles *pfft* and pierce inside you. There is blood where you really don't want blood.

If you're smart, you spend the weekend after on a couch. On

that couch, I watched *Barney Miller*—which aired when I was in high school—with fresh eyes.

First, you see Wojo, a burly young Polish cop, a little baffled and indignant at this changing world. He's negotiating between a lady who's had her purse stolen and a gay pickpocket. But you also notice the space: the walls are worse for wear; the colors are so brown-green you might as well be underwater; the whole place is littered and junky—cubbyholes, pigeonholes, filing cabinets, chalkboards, frosted glass, typewriters and Rolodexes, papers and books, and what appears to be a bowling trophy.

Then the credits: the New York skyline viewed from the bay. A bass sweetly doodles. Horns perk the credits up. You're reunited with the cast: Fish, the man whose body seems to be aging as he speaks; Wojo; the amiable Hispanic Chano (everybody has an ethnic tag). But the person you want to be is Barney Miller. He is the Andy Griffith of his TV generation—the enlightened sheriff.

It's a cop show about paperwork and talk, and the criminals are often charming misfits. The show has the kind of preachy enlightenment that makes *M*A*S*H* reruns almost unwatchable. But it works here.

So, feeling more like old Fish than young Wojo, recently tenderized with needles, afraid to pee, convalescing on the couch, you let yourself reenter this bygone world. And that's the beauty of nostalgia: you really see the world as it existed then. When you're in the present, you see your worries first and foremost, and the world flickers distractedly in the middle ground. Nostalgia can falsify the past, but it can also be the past with the fear and pettiness removed. No other show feels more like the seventies than *Barney Miller,* and despite the bad rap the decade gets, the seventies felt pretty good—tolerant and funny, less full of itself than the sixties. I wish I had seen the decade more clearly.

And, now, in the present, why don't I spend more time dissolving the insistent smudge of self so I can see the world?

I would find out a week later that I was cancer free. I would know the value of seeing the world clearly and living the moment fully. But I would still default to pettiness.

* * *

I can't shake my love of the past. It has hovered on every page of this book. I wanted to let you know how good these people were, how much I loved them, how much I loved our farm and our town and our rock-and-roll records.

And if what I felt about Rollingstone didn't have something to it, this book would be pointless. Or else it would be a clichéd tale of an "artistic" boy's escape from the oppression of small-town life, and God, please spare me from that. I am convinced that the urge to honor my past isn't vacuous, but its deepest impulse is maddeningly simple: *I missed these people; I am sad that they have gone.*

But if I were to elaborate on that simple impulse behind this memoir, if I were to talk about the values I grew up with, what would I talk about? I would celebrate the sacrifices my mother made when she was fueling herself with seventeen cups of coffee, the connection I felt when I joined the rest of the town in cheering my brother's basketball games or when every errand meant encountering friends, the tradition that lifted me when I heard the priest intone the Mass or saw Sister Maureen struggle with my questions, and the humor that buoyed me when my brother and sisters tossed knock-knock jokes and Dad sang "May the Bird of Paradise Fly Up Your Nose." But to isolate those qualities like that is to fillet them into platitudes.

I am thirty-three years old. I haven't had a drink in two years. I have a good if unspectacular job in marketing communications. I am starting to see Ellen socially and will soon see her romantically. I've been rooming with my Winona friend Daryl Lanz, and, when he moves out, I realize I have almost no furniture. I complain to my mom, "I'm a thirty-three-year-old man with no possessions."

She answers back, "So was Jesus."

I try to live up to her disdain of materialism, but I don't do a very good job. I now move in circles where the people I sometimes have to work with often talk disparagingly of anyone who works with his hands, of anyone who does not work in a cube or office, of anyone who does not make as much money as they do. I cringe. I wish I would do more than cringe.

While my mother disdained materialism, she valued work. She worked as a nurse for years. She is in many ways the hero of these pages. When my father died, she found herself fifty and broke and alone, but she never succumbed to any of the dismal emotions that must have tempted her. She kept working. She rebuilt her retirement savings and put together enough that, living humbly, she was able to pay her way through more than a decade of retirement. In that time, she helped at least two of my sisters with college and helped all of her children—except maybe the equally self-sufficient Sheila—when we were financially pressed. *You go to work, you pay your bills, and you help others when you can.* I grew up with her pure, Christian view of work.

My attitude toward work is less pure. A distinction John Lanchester makes in *I.O.U.,* his account of the economic collapse of '08, resonates: he notes a conflict between the values of The City (England's Wall Street) and its industrialists and cites a profound difference between "an industry and a business": "An industry is an entity which as its primary purpose makes or does something and makes money as a by-product." On my good days, I have the values of industry, of craft sometimes focused by profit. I like to make things—even if they are printed, transient things—and acquire things. Among other things, this memoir has been a history of my toys. But my mother's Christian sense of work—as a way of giving service to others, as a way of doing right by God's creation—shadows me.

A year or two later, Ellen and I have decided to live together. I know that Mom's going to oppose it. She may even disown me.

As it is, she has three arguments ready. The first is that living together is too casual, too incremental, for a decision so big. We are wrong if we think the hurt will be somehow less awful if the relationship fails, because it won't be. Her second argument is that "life is complex. If we make moral decisions outside of a moral tradition, we are more likely to delude ourselves." Her third is that "living together is hard. If we undertake a relationship without the support of a community and the grace of a sacrament, we will fail." She has thought about her actions with the precision of a Jesuit. She has, as always, lived up to William James's definition of the spiritual: she had tried to discern and satisfy "the secret demands of the universe." She will not disown me. We are welcome in her apartment. But she will not step into our house while we are living together outside of marriage.

We celebrate Christmas at Sheila's in Minneapolis. Mom gives us a Christmas ornament: two bunnies in a swing with the legend "Our first Christmas together." It is a peace offering. And I think it's important that it is a piece of joyous kitsch, a gesture of my mother's that feels like a gesture of my father's.

The process of writing this memoir has complicated and darkened my view of my father. I'd always mythologized him as a man on a heroic quest to live his destiny, a martyr for the family farm. But now I see strains of his human imperfection: there was something selfish and prideful about his insistence on returning to the farm when we lived in Rollingstone. By that time, Dennis was already exhausted from trying to do a man's job. The kids were happier in the house in town, and, because the farm wasn't draining cash, the family was more prosperous and less besieged.

That said, I enjoy an inheritance from my family that has little to do with my mother: the capacity to have fun. Shaped by 1930s Catholicism, my mom has told me that she distrusts fun. She has insisted that struggle is the essence of life. In its way, this is reassuring. If struggle is the essence of life, pain has a point;

struggle is often the fizzing beaker of insight. But when I look back at my childhood, I think that celebration is also the point of life—that God likes Paul Revere and the Raiders songs and board games and knock-knock jokes and sitcoms and basketball games and riding pickup trucks fast over farm roads. God did not create the world just to bum us out.

My dad's love of fun influenced us even after he was gone. When Ellen and I were getting married, there was about a week there when it wasn't clear Mom would be attending. She wasn't happy about our decision to get married in the Episcopal Church. She came around in a few days—I think after talking to priests in Winona—but Colleen told me that, like a president arming nuclear weapons, my sister was ready to "play the Dad card," a tactic that no one had ever actually employed. To wit, Colleen was ready to say to Mom, "Dad would be there. Dad never missed a party."

My values are Rollingstone and Winona, but my life has been lived in Minneapolis–St. Paul. The life of my friend Bill Schuth suggests what my life might have been like had I not gone to the Cities. If *The Bob Newhart Show* was my template, *The Andy Griffith Show* was Bill's. (Yes, the influence of sitcoms on my life is a little disturbing.) Bill stayed in the Winona area—first selling insurance in Lake City, Minnesota, for a few years and then, after a failed first marriage (we all suffered and stumbled in our twenties), settling into Trempealeau, Wisconsin—a river town south of Winona—for close to thirty years, where he taught first junior high and then high school. A curious man with a quick intellect, he taught math, English, and even a film course, touching hundreds of lives. He had a mind that was hard to change but easy to engage. He and his wife, Judy, had three children, and they co-parented his older child, Bill.

I rarely regret the decision to not have a family. But I felt a pang the evening I visited the Schuths for a dinner that resembled the farm dinners I grew up on—roasted meat, butter pooling in mashed potatoes, bright corn, white bread and butter, Folgers coffee with Kemps ice cream—and I helped Bill's grade school-age sons with their homework and admired the stuffed animals his preschool daughter presented me. I marveled at the warmth and light of the home Bill and Judy had created. It was the warmth and light my parents, for a few fragile years, had created for us.

At thirty-seven, Bill joined the local volunteer fire department and eventually became a captain. He taught Sunday school. It was a life in which he kept circling back to help others—as a teacher, as a father, as a firefighter—and in this circling back, he found meaning and happiness.

And he did all this without letting his opinions calcify, even when he was faced with a death sentence. When we met for lunch in Winona in our late forties, Bill told me that some cancer that he thought was in remission was back and that it had returned virulently. The doctors gave him a 50 percent chance of living two years and a 5 percent chance of living five years. He beat the two-year mark, and, for a brief time, the cancer seemed to have abated.

He remained Bill. His soul was still decent, and his mind was still vigorous. He had resentments—we all do—but he never let them metastasize. We talked about politics—health care, teachers' unions, even gay marriage—and our discussions were free of the rancor and reflexivity of most political talk. I think we both shared a sense that we had been lucky men, and we wanted to make sure that the next generations had our opportunities.

He stayed curious. He asked me to help him remember sitcom episodes. He recommended diners with spectacular burgers or pies. He pointed me to favorite bluegrass or rockabilly music. He asked that I send a draft of this manuscript down to him as he was convalescing so he could have something to do now that he no longer taught school or fought fires.

We talked about prayer. I shared with him something that former drunks like to say: *My creator, I am now willing for you to have all of me, good and bad. I pray that you remove from me every single defect of character which stands in the way of my usefulness to you and my fellows. Grant me strength, as I go out from here, to do thy will.* He leaned across the booth at the Country Kitchen and said, "That's fantastic." As he was dying, he prayed for his children.

But then I received an e-mail as I sat in the Beloit College campus, having returned to my alma mater for classroom visits and a reading. My happiness was already thickened with a wistful gratefulness. The campus was green with spring, a green intensified by overcast skies. I was returning with something to show for myself, a novel that finally bore fruit from the years I had spent at Beloit—a place I've rarely written of partly because it was a happy time and partly because this is the place where I came to learn how to write about Minnesota.

I had realized that—despite the cheese strata at commons and the usual romantic disappointments and the drinking that would in a few years tip into alcoholism—spending four years at a private liberal arts college where one's *work* consisted of reading and thinking and talking with friends on these beautiful grounds is as close to paradise as one gets on this earth. I'd been editor of the *Beloit College Round Table,* and I was staring up at where our offices used to be, a cluttered attic room where we used to hack out copy on IBM Selectrics and physically cut and paste stories into layout. I was already missing the people I'd worked with. I hadn't realized at the time that sensations I had taken for granted—the rotation and punch of typewriter ball on ribbon on paper, the delicate blades of X-Acto knives, and the tackiness of the paste we applied to the thick stories—were about to become antique.

And I did not realize as I sat down on that bench on the Beloit campus that, in the e-mail I was about to open, my friend would describe how, in four days he would die:

I am sorry that delivering this information will be so blunt. It's tough news and there's no good way to tell it.

Yesterday, the oncologist said that when I go on hospice (today), the amount of time I have left would be measured in days. Not long. He said that because it was a liver problem, I would get sleepy, confused, and then fall into a sleep. I would sleep for a few days, in a coma-like situation, which would not allow me to be awakened, and then I would pass away. Sounds like a relatively gentle ending.

Except for one last trip to the shrine this afternoon, I hope to stay around the house from now on.

–Bill

Bill Schuth died too young. He would have been the world's greatest grandpa. But he lived well. In the next few days, his house would fill with visitors. On Easter Sunday, as he lay dying and filled with morphine, his siblings prayed around him. They wept. They asked him if there was anyone else he would like to see. He quipped, "*Dick Van Dyke.*" Death would get to him before self-pity did.

Later that week, I arrived at the funeral ten minutes early, and I couldn't find a seat. Friends and family packed the church, and a parade of fire trucks led mourners to his grave.

When I saw on a *Batman* rerun a few months later that one of the high schools in Gotham was named Disko Tech, I thought, *I have to tell Bill about this,* and then I realized he was dead. I have pangs like this all the time, and I imagine I always will.

Cynical politicians will talk about the real America—and they're referring to places like Trempealeau and lives like Bill's. Of course, the whole damn country from Park Slope to Rollingstone to West Hollywood is all real. But there are possibilities for a life well lived that villages nourish and cities disperse. Still, some of us choose the city.

The movie trailer I play in my head—my family at breakfast in the kitchen on the farm—is set in 1966. In 1966, my father was forty-five. He and Mom had five children to support. He had lost his farm once. Multiple hip replacements had failed. His medical bills were in the hundreds of thousands. The latest replacement complained in his body, and he sensed that it, too, would not last.

As I first draft this sentence, I am forty-five. I am a freelance copywriter, and my business is prospering. Other than some occasional back pain that traces from a tennis game several months ago, I am healthy. Because Ellen and I have no children, I'm able to fit graduate school in the margins of my life. I don't own a lawn, much less a farm. In our condo, we look out our third-story window into the top of a tree. It is green in summer, calligraphic in winter.

I fantasized a particular life when I stayed at the Thunderbird Motel and when I watched Bob Newhart. My life is closer to those fantasies than I ever imagined it would be. I work in the city, as a writer. I live in a condominium, in a building that had once been a hotel. If I cared to, I could walk to watch Minnesota's professional hockey team. (Sports is now an occasional entertainment for me, not a passion.) My life today is much easier than my parents' ever was. When Ellen and I sink into the couch on a Friday night with our greyhound, Albert, snoozing in front of us and let swinging sixties reruns—*The Avengers, The Saint*—wash over us, I am almost inappropriately happy. Tomorrow, this could all change. A cigarette—or more likely, today, a cell phone—could be dropped, a car could explode.

My visit to the Thunderbird Motel was more prophetic than I could have imagined. And, upon reflection, it reveals something about me. As I conceived this book, I thought that, in sixth grade, I contemplated the glowing Rollingstone school with a sense of impending loss. But I now don't believe that is what I was feeling, at least not exactly.

I felt something that would be reawakened again years later when I stood in front of that lighted pizza place before meeting with Neal, and then, in the mid-nineties, when I would stand in a parking lot in downtown Minneapolis on First Avenue, looking at the stream of rush hour traffic pouring down the street like a procession of candles. I gazed at the purple dusk and then upward at the illuminated windows of the advertising agency where I worked. A few people were still working, and I realized that this was where I always wanted to be—that this was what Petula Clark was singing about when she sang "Downtown." That is where I felt what Fitzgerald's Dutch sailor felt in *The Great Gatsby*—and this may say something about the smallness of my capacities—when Nick Carraway contemplated that "for a transitory enchanted moment man must have held his breath in the presence of this continent . . . face to face . . . with something commensurate with his capacity for wonder." I did not face a continent. In 1970, I faced a school. In the 1990s, I faced an office building. I was within a few blocks of where Mary Tyler Moore tossed her tam o'shanter in the air.

But in another sense, I did face a continent—the luminous island of American culture, of millions of magazines and television shows and movies and records and books.

What I was feeling as I looked at Rollingstone Elementary School was not a loss but a foreshadowing. Even if Dad had lived, even if the surgeries had succeeded, and even if the school had survived, I was going to leave Rollingstone. My sadness is more petty, or at least more complicated, than I thought. I wanted to break up with Rollingstone before it broke up with me.

But I am also closer to my past than ever before. I live in a city, but, after two years in an anonymous residential neighborhood, we moved back to an urban village—a place where we know the baristas at the coffeehouse, the people who carry treats for our dog, the cashiers at the grocery store. We live in a neighborhood brightened by businesses and foot traffic and sidewalk tables. We live in a place where people recognize you, just as they did in Rollingstone.

And just as I did when I was eight and looked out of my room, into trees, I see a treetop now as I look out our window. Through the treetops, I can see the neon signs of a bar. It is the kind of place my dad would have liked. It is the kind of place I once sought out before I realized that I had spent too much of my adult life wanting too much from things—wanting the remembered past to be the actual present, wanting places to be as loving as people and people to be as stable as places, wanting the chemical to be the spiritual.

I may not live here forever. The demands of the market, the negotiations of marriage, and the inevitable shifts in my own situation might direct me somewhere else. But I feel as if I've arrived at one of the destinations I was supposed to reach.

I've heard the urge to write described with the Biblical invocation, *I alone have escaped to tell thee.* The word *escaped* is important. At first, it seems to propel us frenetically forward. But it defines us by what we have abandoned.

ACKNOWLEDGMENTS

AN EXCERPT FROM *LEAVING ROLLINGSTONE* APPEARED IN *The Gettysburg Review.*

* * *

In a sense, *Leaving Rollingstone* is a book-length acknowledgements section.

Thanks to my brother and sisters and all the classmates, friends, and grown-ups in Rollingstone, Minnesota City, and Winona, named and unnamed, who made growing up in those places worth writing about.

To my many thoughtful readers: Joanna Johnson, Tom Kendrick, Nan Fulle, Sarah Sawyer, Joe Hart, Carolyn Crooke, Jon Spayde, Esther Porter, Sari Fordham, Josh Labau, Marisha Chamberlain, Ric James, and Greg Schaffner

To Patricia Hampl and her crazy-good thesis prep class—Bryan Bradford, Amy Shearn, Matt Duffus, Marge Barrett, Kate Hopper, Will Bush, Joseph Laizure, and Amanda Fields.

For their generous support of me as a writer and friend: Dan O'Shea, Mike Schwartz, Larry Nowlin, Dave Hultgren, Jill

Crosby, Marc Schiapacasse, Joel Turnipseed, Joe Isaak, Steve Collins, Dan Munson, Pat Marcotte, Dave Curle, Miriam Hollar, Daryl Lanz, and Dawn Bentley.

To Mimi Sprengnether and Charlie Sugnet of the Minnesota MFA program.

To the Anderson Center in Red Wing, Minnesota, where I made some significant progress on this manuscript in what might be the perfect environment for writing.

To the Winona County History Society, who graciously pointed me to resources.

To everyone at the Minnesota Historical Society Press: Shannon Pennefeather, Alison Aten, and freelancer Thomas Dean.

And especially to Tom McBride, Chrissy Kolaya, Cheri Johnson, and Pamela McClanahan, who saw a better book inside my manuscript than I did.

LEAVING ROLLINGSTONE
was designed and set in type by Judy Gilats in St. Paul, Minnesota. The text face is Turnip and the display face is Goshen. The book was printed by Edwards Brothers Malloy, Ann Arbor, Michigan.

Printed in the USA
CPSIA information can be obtained
at www.ICGtesting.com
JSHW082203140824
68134JS00014B/404